WHA[barcode]

and other Marine Mammals of
WASHINGTON
and
OREGON

Tamara Eder

illustrations by
Ian Sheldon

with technical contributions from
Don Pattie

LONE PINE

Lone Pine Publishing

The Publisher: Lone Pine Publishing
1901 Raymond Ave. SW, Suite C
Renton, WA 98055
USA
Website: http://www.lonepinepublishing.com

10145 – 81 Ave.
Edmonton, AB T6E 1W9
Canada

National Library of Canada Cataloguing in Publication Data

Eder, Tamara (date)
    Whales and other marine mammals of Washington and Oregon

    Includes bibliographical references and index.
    ISBN 1-55105-266-0

    1. Whales—Washington (State)—Identification. 2. Whales—Oregon—
Identification. 3. Marine mammals—Washington (State)—Identification.
4. Marine mammals—Oregon—Identification. I. Sheldon, Ian, (date) II. Title.
QL737.C4E238 2001   599.4'09795   C2001-910417-0

Editorial Director: Nancy Foulds
Project Editor: Roland Lines
Technical Review: Ian McCaskie
Production Manager: Jody Reekie
Cover Design: Robert Weidemann
Book Design: Robert Weidemann
Layout & Production: Ian Dawe
Cartography: Robert Weidemann, Ian Dawe
Cover Illustrations: Humpback Whale & Gray Whale, by Ian Sheldon
Separations & Film: Elite Lithographers Co.

Photography Credits
The photographs in this book are reproduced with the generous permission of their copyright holders.
Ken Balcomb, pp. 40 & 88; Corel Corporation (photos by Eric Stoops), pp. 44, 52, 68, 72, 92 & 108; Renee DeMartin/West Stock, pp. 56, 82 & 124; Tamara Eder, pp. 120 & 132; Eyewire, p. 116; Mark Newman/West Stock, p. 128; Marty Snyderman/Visuals Unlimited, p. 60.

Additional Illustrations
The illustrations of the two otters (pp. 130 & 134) are by Gary Ross.

We acknowledge the financial support of the Government of Canada through the Book Publishing Industry Development Program (BPIDP) for our publishing activities.

PC: P4

For my grandmother, Irene Louise Carnegie Savage,
for her devotion to her family and the inspiring tales of her own (mis)adventures.

Contents

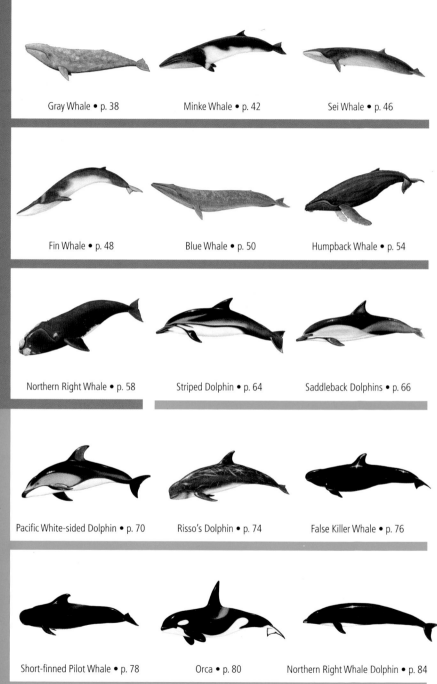

BALEEN WHALES

Gray Whale • p. 38

Minke Whale • p. 42

Sei Whale • p. 46

Fin Whale • p. 48

Blue Whale • p. 50

Humpback Whale • p. 54

Northern Right Whale • p. 58

Striped Dolphin • p. 64

Saddleback Dolphins • p. 66

TOOTHED WHALES

Pacific White-sided Dolphin • p. 70

Risso's Dolphin • p. 74

False Killer Whale • p. 76

Short-finned Pilot Whale • p. 78

Orca • p. 80

Northern Right Whale Dolphin • p. 84

Harbor Porpoise • p. 86   Dall's Porpoise • p. 90   Baird's Beaked Whale • p. 94

Cuvier's Beaked Whale • p. 96   Hubbs's Beaked Whale • p. 98   Stejneger's Beaked Whale • p. 100

Pygmy Sperm Whale • p. 102   Dwarf Sperm Whale • p. 104   Sperm Whale • p. 106

Northern
Fur Seal • p. 112

Northern
Sea-Lion • p. 114

California
Sea-Lion • p. 118

Harbor Seal
p. 122

Northern Elephant Seal • p. 126   Sea Otter • p. 130   Northern River Otter • p. 134

Introduction

In 1969, we saw Earth from the moon. During the first moon landing, pictures of our planet were radioed back to Earth for everyone to see. These first images of Earth kindled a new kind of enlightenment and shifted our awareness of ourselves and our place on the planet. Seeing images of "Spaceship Earth" sparked two (among many) profound realizations that not only affected our thinking at the time, but would eventually affect the relationship between humans and whales. Primarily, the images reminded us that Earth is dominated by oceans. More than 70 percent of our planet's surface is covered by water, and the creatures that thrive in the marine habitat are marvelous in their form and adaptation. The second realization, rather less obvious, is that we may not be alone in this universe, and we conjured up a keen anticipation of finding non-human intelligence. One result of these combined realizations was a new appreciation for those animals that live in the sea, and when we looked into the eyes of whales and saw something familiar and hopefully intelligent, we redoubled our efforts to understand and protect these great creatures.

Whales have fascinated people for thousands of years. At least 3500 years ago, the early Greeks used images of dolphins on mosaics, frescos, vases and coins. Aristotle is believed to be the first person to propose that whales and dolphins are mammals, not fish, and he correctly identified and classified several different species.

When people speak of whales, they generally imagine the large whales that live in deep oceans. Broadly speaking, the distinction between whales, dolphins and porpoises is based on size rather than zoological affinity: whales are typically the largest of the three; porpoises are the smallest. Some of the largest dolphins are larger than the smallest whales, however, so the terminology can be confusing. Technically, whales include the Gray Whale, rorquals, Bowhead Whale, right whales, Beluga, Narwhal, sperm whales and beaked whales. Dolphins include the Orca, pilot whales, ocean dolphins and river dolphins. Many people call the Orca the Killer Whale, but it is really the largest member of the dolphin family. There are only six species of porpoises worldwide.

All whales, dolphins and porpoises are members of the order Cetacea, and they are commonly called "cetaceans." They are distinguished from other mammals by their nearly hairless bodies, paddle-like forelimbs, lack of hindlimbs, fusiform bodies and powerful tail flukes. At least 81 species of cetaceans are known to exist today, and they are scientifically classified into two suborders according to whether they have baleen or teeth. The baleen whales are in the suborder Mysticeti and the toothed whales are in the suborder Odontoceti. There are only 11 species of baleen whales worldwide. They are the rorqual whales, Gray Whale, Bowhead Whale and right whales. The toothed whales number at least 70 species worldwide, including porpoises, dolphins, sperm whales, the Narwhal, the Beluga and beaked whales.

About This Guide

No matter where you are learning about whales, whether aboard a whale-watching boat on the ocean or in the comfort of your own home, keep this book handy for quick reference about whales and other marine mammals. All the species you might encounter off the coasts of Washington and Oregon are illustrated and described within this book. As well, historical and biological information is presented to give you a better understanding about whales in general.

About 25 whale species occur in the waters off Washington and Oregon. Of these, 7 are baleen whales (mysticetes) and 18 are toothed whales (odontocetes). The most famous and commonly seen cetaceans in this region are the Gray Whale, Humpback Whale, Orca and Harbor Porpoise, but less common cetaceans may be encountered at any time.

The whales of Washington and Oregon are presented here in a generally accepted sequence that places the more closely related whales near one another. The scientific names and the ordering of the groups (genera) and species follow the "Revised checklist of North American mammals north of Mexico, 1997" (Occasional Paper No. 173, Museum of Texas Tech University, by Jones, Hoffmann, Rice et al. 1997). The section describing the other marine mammals in the region is similarly ordered, but placed after the section on whales. The common names used in this book are widely accepted and frequently used names. Owing to discrepancies in the common names of many species, however, some species may be found under different names in other texts. Wherever necessary, the alternate common names are included in each entry as well as in the index.

The quick reference guide on pages 4 and 5 illustrates all the species in the book. It may help you identify species and groups at a glance, and it leads you to the detailed descriptions of each species. The blows and dive sequences for selected species are also illustrated together on pages 22 and 23. The glossary (pp. 136–37) defines some of the specialized terms that are used in talking about whales, and it also includes labeled diagrams of the main cetacean bodyparts.

Each species account includes a "Status" entry, giving information on the current conservation status of the species. Descriptions such as "endangered," "threatened" and "vulnerable" are official designations made by the U.S. Fish and Wildlife Service (FWS) and are defined in the glossary. Other descriptions appearing in the book, such as "common," "stable" or "declining," are used in accordance with current local research.

It should be noted that the lifecycles of many whales are described in terms of the animal's size, instead of its age. Because of our limited understanding of cetaceans, we are unable to estimate an individual's age for most species, whereas length can be readily measured in the field.

The "Similar Species" section in each account lists other whales or marine mammals that could easily be confused with the whale you are reading about. Be sure to check the descriptions of these other species before you decide on the identity of a whale in the wild.

Once you have learned to identify whales, and you are familiar with their natural history, enjoy them! Whales are marvelous creatures and watching them can be a thrilling and memorable experience.

Whale Watching

Whale watching has become a worldwide activity that attracts millions of people each year. The coasts of Washington and Oregon have many famous sites where whale watchers can easily see Orcas and Gray, Humpback and Minke whales. Other species that can be seen unexpectedly at any time are Blue, Fin, Sei and Sperm whales. As for smaller species, Pacific White-sided Dolphins and Dall's and Harbor porpoises can be seen in certain locations. The preceding species are the most frequently seen whales, but remember that every species in this book can be found in the waters of Washington and Oregon. Keep your eyes open for the rarer whales—positive sightings are worth reporting to local research stations.

The west coast of North America has some of the most exciting places in the world for viewing and studying whales. Despite past whaling and current heavy boat traffic, the harbors, straits and food-rich waters of our coast form prime habitat for many species of whales. Gray Whales perform their long migrations along this coast, and some of the best-known and most-studied populations of Orcas and Humpbacks also inhabit these waters.

While it is true that you may encounter whales throughout the coastal regions of Washington and Oregon, some places are better than others to find whales. The map on the facing page illustrates the best sites for whale watching, which also correlates to good availability of whale-watching tours. With respect, the places where whales are sensitive to disturbance or places that are ecologically fragile have not been included. Nevertheless, some of the best whale-watching sites in the world are here, ready for you to explore.

The sheltered water of Washington's Puget Sound is an excellent location to see certain cetaceans all year. Many species, especially Orcas and the smaller dolphins and porpoises, enjoy the sheltered, food-rich water there. Heavy boat traffic is a concern, but so far, the whale populations are healthy.

Water characteristics and the availability of food are also important factors determining whale density. From central Oregon northward, the North Pacific Current and the Alaska

Current circulate cold, nutrient-rich water from the deep ocean bottom. Animal and plant life is abundant because of this upwelling, and many species of animals grow larger there than their relatives do in less-rich water elsewhere. Planktonic invertebrates are extremely abundant, and they feed the large baleen whales. Fish are also abundant in the cold water, and they

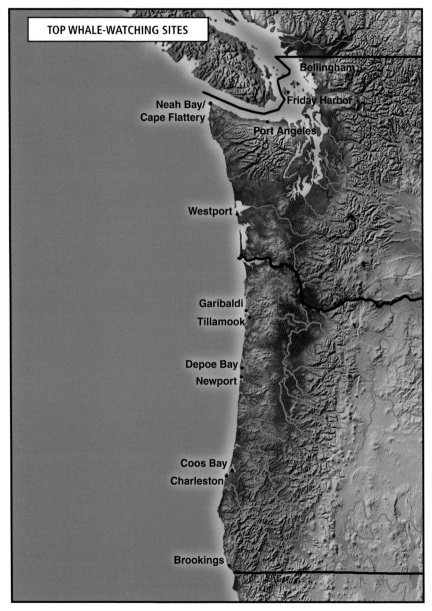

TOP WHALE-WATCHING SITES

Bellingham

Neah Bay/
Cape Flattery

Friday Harbor

Port Angeles

Westport

Garibaldi
Tillamook

Depoe Bay
Newport

Coos Bay
Charleston

Brookings

become food for the toothed whales, seals and sea-lions. The ocean currents off southern Oregon and northern California are warmer, and although several species can be found year-round there, many of the migratory baleen whales just pass through those waters without stopping. They are headed for even warmer waters off southern California and Mexico.

There are many choices to make if you are to have a successful whale-watching adventure. The time of year is important: catching the peak of migration makes for the best chances of seeing certain species. Some species, such as Orcas, can be seen year-round, although they are much less common in winter. If you want to take a boat tour, you can choose between a day trip or a multiple-day cruise. Costs vary depending on how long a trip you are taking.

Always research who is operating the tour. A tour leader should be knowledgeable of whale biology and up to date on the current locations of different whales. It is essential that the tour operator is responsible and behaves ethically around whales. Like people, whales have personalities and personal space requirements, and boaters that harass whales (even unknowingly) can be extremely disruptive to the animal and can cause unnecessary stress and harm. In the worst cases, a whale that is badly harassed may show aggression towards boaters and can suffer stress or injuries. In the best cases, a whale may be comfortable with your presence and approach your boat on its own accord to get a better look at you. If you are the skipper of your own boat, know the basic guidelines for approaching whales. The most stringent and concise rules on the West Coast are those from Alaska:

- Minimum approach distance is 300 ft (91 m).
- Approach or leave whales at "no-wake" speed from the side or behind (never from ahead) with no sudden changes in speed or direction.
- If a whale approaches, put the engine in neutral and allow it to pass.
- Never follow whales or herd, drive or separate them, particularly mothers and calves.
- Only one vessel at a time at the minimum approach distance.
- There is a time limit of 30 minutes per vessel at the minimum distance.
- Swimmers should not approach within 150 ft (46 m).

The Marine Mammal Protection Act of 1972 prohibits the harassing, capturing or killing of any marine mammal. Anyone breaking this law is subject to fines of up to $25,000 or imprisonment. Most tour operators are knowledgeable, responsible and show genuine concern for the welfare of whales. If you encounter people who are not following proper conduct around whales, please speak up. Let them know they are interfering with and possibly harming the whales. If everyone acts responsibly, the whales will probably stay in the vicinity for everyone to enjoy.

The industry of whale watching is more than just the intrinsic pleasure of seeing these great creatures. On the West Coast, from Alaska to Oregon, whale watching brings in at least $5 million each year. The accessory items related to whale watching are an additional $2 million to $3 million, at least. To look at whale watching in monetary terms is important if whale conservation is to be politically and economically acceptable. On the other hand, attaching dollar figures to whale watching is superficial at best. How can we put a dollar figure on awe-inspiring experiences in the wild? As every whale watcher knows, the true value is in the extraordinary and breathtaking encounter with a wild whale.

Whale Origins and Evolution

The evolutionary history of whales is truly remarkable. Mammals originated on land, so cetaceans must have arisen from terrestrial ancestors. In fact, their closest living relatives are the artiodactyls: even-toed hoofed mammals such as cattle, antelopes, pigs and hippopotamuses. The artiodactyls and the cetaceans have common ancestors that are unlike either of these present-day groups.

Mammals existed as early as 210 million years ago, but the great dinosaurs dominated the world until 65 million years ago, and mammals remained very small and insignificant. After the dinosaurs died out, mammals had the chance to diversify, and they evolved to walk the earth, fly in the sky and swim in the oceans. The first ancestor of whales known through fossil finds is likely 50-million-year-old Ambulocetus, an amphibious, dolphin-sized mammal that had hindlegs with webbed feet for swimming. Ambulocetus probably gave rise to Pakicetus, which still had legs, but had a more whale-like skull, teeth, jaw and tail stock. By the early Oligocene (34 million years ago) several toothed whales existed, and Mammalodon, the baleen whale ancestor, also appeared. Once the basic physiology was established, cetaceans diversified dramatically, and by about 7 million years ago, the major forms of whales, dolphins and porpoises that we recognize today had evolved.

Pakicetus

Over millions of years of evolution, the body plan of the whale changed dramatically from a four-legged progenitor to the streamlined oceanic form we see today. The loss of the hindlimbs and the modification of the forelimbs into flippers with no moving elbows are striking changes to the basic mammalian plan. Whales still retain a vestigial pelvis and femur, because selective pressure for eliminating such structures is weak. The blowhole originated from the nostrils, which migrated to the top of the head and effectively separated breathing and eating. The ears were modified for hearing underwater, and echolocation developed in the toothed whales. The dorsal line of the whale adapted to create better propulsion underwater: the neck vertebrae stiffened, a dorsal fin originated, muscles and bones along the tail stock strengthened, and the tail flukes developed. Skulls and jaws were highly modified, and about 33 to 34 million years ago, the division between baleen and toothed whales occurred. This division was paramount, because the baleen whales became specialized for catching large quantities of small creatures, while the toothed whales could catch smaller quantities of larger prey. Other modified features include a highly streamlined body and a nearly total loss of body hair.

Although whales and dolphins evolved in the oceans, some species now live in fresh water. The river dolphins, which number five species worldwide, inhabit large river systems, such as the Amazon, Orinoco, Indus, Ganges and Yangtze. As well, most porpoises can travel freely between fresh and salt water, as can the Beluga. Generally speaking, however, the salt-water whales tire quickly in fresh water (because of their reduced buoyancy), and their skin might wrinkle and slough (just like ours does in a bath).

The fact that whales look a bit like sharks is a tribute to convergent evolution. Sharks and whales are not closely related at all, and there are many physiological differences between them, but their similar appearance reflects a desirable body plan for being a successful ocean creature. A gray-colored shark and a dolphin, for example, may be difficult to distinguish at first glance.

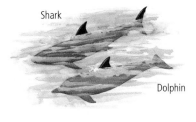

Although mammals have many characteristics that differentiate them from other animals, the most obvious differences between whales and sharks are that whales breathe air and nurse their young, while sharks have gills and do not nurse their young. The easiest way to distinguish between sharks and whales, however, is to look at their tails: the flukes of a cetacean are horizontal; the tail of a shark is vertical. Many frightened swimmers have thought an approaching dolphin was a shark, but a shark swimming close to the surface of the water reveals two triangular "fins" above the surface: its dorsal fin and the top of its tail. Dolphins, on the other hand, only reveal their dorsal fin.

Behavior and Adaptations

FEEDING WITH BALEEN

The baleen whales, or mysticetes, are typically the largest of all cetaceans. Of these, the largest are the females. Ironically, these large whales feed on some of the tiniest ocean creatures.

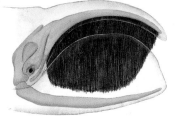

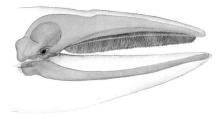

Baleen specialized for skim-feeding
(Bowhead Whale)

Baleen specialized for lunge-feeding
(Minke Whale)

Baleen plates are a remarkable new mammalian adaptation that permits efficient filter-feeding of plankton, tiny crustaceans, small fish and some mollusks from the ocean water. Baleen was once called "whalebone," but it is really not bone at all. Although baleen grows where teeth normally would on other mammals, it is actually made of an entirely different keratinous material very similar to human fingernails and hair. The baleen plates grow down from the gum of the upper jaw, and they are shaped like very long, narrow triangles. All the plates hang one against the other, similar to vertical blinds on a livingroom window. The hairs on the edge of each plate face into the mouth.

Lunge-feeding, also known as gulp-feeding, and skim-feeding are the two basic styles of feeding among baleen whales. Within each style, there is variation between species and even individuals.

The rorqual whales primarily use lunge-feeding. If necessary, prior to lunging, the whale herds its prey into a tight group near the surface. Once the prey is concentrated, the whale lunges and opens its mouth to gulp in tons of food-rich water. A rorqual has

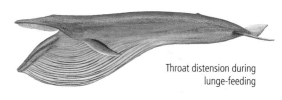

Throat distension during
lunge-feeding

specialized throat pleats that expand like an accordion and allow the throat to distend to balloon-like dimensions. These pleats contract automatically as the whale closes its gaping mouth. The mouth is not closed completely, but just enough to permit the baleen to meet the lower jaw and create a sieve. The water is squeezed out through the baleen, while the krill, copepods and other small creatures are trapped inside the mouth against the baleen. Rorquals have short baleen that is continuous around the front of the jaw, making the mouth an effective filter when it is nearly closed.

A famous variation of lunge-feeding is when Humpback Whales use bubble-netting. One or several Humpbacks begin releasing bubbles as they swim in a circle below a school of fish. As the bubbles rise, they create a curtain that disorients the fish and traps them in a central area. Once the fish are sufficiently concentrated inside this bubble-net, the whales surge up in the middle of the "net" and gulp the creatures into their gaping mouths.

Skim-feeding is passive by comparison to lunge-feeding, and it is a style utilized primarily by right whales. The Sei Whale, although it is a rorqual, frequently uses skim-feeding, as well.

Humpback Whale bubble-netting

For a long time, skim-feeding was believed to occur at or near the surface, simply because we could see the whales doing it there. Skim-feeding often occurs at great depths, however, and only recently was this activity recorded on film by researchers. This feeding style requires the whale to swim through a school of plankton or other small creatures with its mouth open.

Right whales do not have any baleen at the front of their mouths, and the baleen on the sides is very long. As a result, when the whale opens its mouth, the opening is like a small cave with walls of baleen. As the whale swims through the food-rich water, the water enters the mouth and continues right out through the baleen. Food also goes into the mouth, but it is trapped by the long baleen. The throats of these whales do not extend, and the mouth is kept still and open as the whale swims. Once many food creatures have accumulated in the mouth, the whale closes its jaws and swallows.

Northern Right Whale skim-feeding

FEEDING WITH TEETH

The toothed whales feed on creatures larger than those fed on by baleen whales. Their jaws are modified depending on their style of feeding and their prey. Dolphins, for example, often have long, narrow jaws that are fast-closing and capable of catching small, darting fish. Orcas, on the other hand, have wider jaws with heavy, conical teeth for holding prey and tearing off large chunks. The size of its prey matters little to the Orca, and certain groups of Orcas are known to regularly attack other cetaceans, such as porpoises, dolphins and even larger whales, especially sick or injured ones. Porpoises have spade-shaped teeth that are flattened side to side. These teeth are effective for slicing and shearing, rather than holding prey.

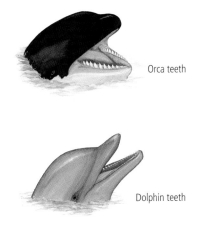

Orca teeth

Dolphin teeth

The Sperm Whale and the beaked whales are believed to be suction feeders—by quickly moving the tongue backward in the mouth, they create a powerful suction to pull in their prey—and there is much debate about how useful teeth are to them. The Sperm Whale has a very narrow jaw, relative to the size of its head, with heavy, conical teeth. The white mouth of the Sperm Whale may even act like a lure to bring its prey close. One adult Sperm Whale that was killed had no lower jaw at all—an astonishing injury that appeared to have little effect on the overall health of the whale, which was large and clearly well-fed.

Beaked whales have some of the strangest teeth and jaws of all the toothed whales. Usually, only the male's teeth erupt, while the females feed without any functional teeth. Males have two teeth (sometimes four) in the lower jaw, either close to the tip of the beak or in the middle. The teeth tend to be large and triangular shaped, and sometimes they overlap the upper jaw on the outside of the mouth.

THE BLOWHOLE

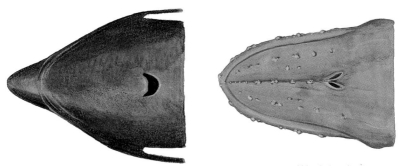

Single blowhole of toothed whales

Paired blowholes of baleen whales

One of the marvels of cetacean anatomy is the blowhole. Unable to breathe through its mouth, a whale inhales and exhales exclusively through its blowhole. The blowhole is designed for rapid air exchange, and it is the result of an evolutionary change in skull shape and a slow migration of the nostrils and breathing passage to the top of the head—away from the throat. In some cases, most notably the Humpback Whale, air can voluntarily be released from the lungs into the mouth if the trachea is slightly dislodged, but this action does not give the whale the ability to breathe through its mouth.

For whales, breathing is voluntary, and they open and close their blowholes at will. The baleen whales have two blowholes that are controlled by strong muscles attached to the upper jaw. When they surface, they make an explosive blow and inhale in such quick succession that the entire process takes only a few seconds. The toothed whales appear to have only one blowhole. In fact, they have two nasal passages, each

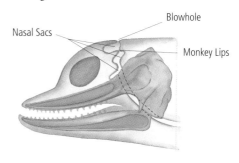

with the ability to open and close, but these passages are hidden internally and called "monkey lips." The single, external blowhole is a new adaptation unique to toothed whales that allows for sound generation by the hidden soft tissues of the nasal passages.

SLEEP

Unlike terrestrial mammals, cetaceans do not enter a deep state of sleep. They must rest, but they require much less sleep than other mammals. Evidence suggests that whales require less sleep because the marine environment induces a brain state that resembles sleep. Even humans, when in water for prolonged periods, may require only one hour of sleep a day where they otherwise would sleep eight hours. Moreover, whales are voluntary breathers, and in order for them to breathe at the surface, to keep moving to prevent stranding and to watch for potential dangers, the whales must never fall soundly asleep. Dolphins and porpoises are able to "sleep" half their brain at a time.

To relax, many whales use the technique of "logging" at the surface. Logging is a form of rest where one or more whales float almost motionless at the surface, all pointing in the same direction. Their breathing and heart rates are lowered, and their eyes may close, but they have not totally lost consciousness. Mariners once believed that a logging whale was fast asleep and even an approaching boat could not wake it, but the opposite is true.

LUNGS AND DIVING

Perhaps the greatest danger for a deep-diving air breather is nitrogen narcosis, a desensitized state caused from pressurized air entering the circulation system. The other hazard is called the bends, where bubbles spontaneously form in joints and tissues from rising to the surface too fast. Whales are not affected by either of these conditions because of several adaptations that evolved over time.

Before a deep dive, whales remove the air from their lungs. Air is highly compressible, whereas water is not. Like our bodies, most of a whale's body is water and can therefore handle the pressure of a dive. Only the air in the lungs is subject to compression. Any air that remains in a whale's lungs is pushed into the inflexible windpipe where it cannot be compressed. This

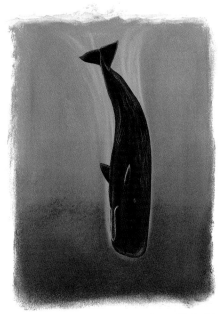

Sperm Whale diving

strategy prevents air compression and thereby effectively eliminates nitrogen narcosis. The bends, also known as decompression sickness, is prevented by the efficient and rapid transport of nitrogen back into the lungs as the whale surfaces. Circulation of blood through the muscles during the dive is also reduced, which further reduces the possibility of bubbles of nitrogen forming.

SOUNDS AND SONGS

In water, sound travels almost five times faster than in air. A cetacean uses sound to keep in touch with other members of its group, and some of the odontocetes use sound for echolocation. Different whales make different sounds, and if the sounds have meaning, one species likely cannot understand those of another species. Sounds vary from loud to quiet, and from deep rumbles and belches to high squeaks and clicks.

Baleen whales commonly produce the deepest and loudest sounds. The vocalizations of a Blue Whale can be less than 20 hertz in frequency and up to 188 decibels in volume. Sophisticated military technology capable of detecting submarine sounds from far away has been able to pick up the sounds of a Blue Whale from over 1500 mi (2400 km) away.

This kind of evidence changes how we look at a group of whales. Perhaps whales do not have to be in visual range to be considered part of the same group. Two rorqual whales seen 30 mi (48 km) apart may not be "solo" whales. Humpback Whales make extremely loud and long songs. Samples of the unique and complex songs of Humpbacks have even been sent out on Voyagers 1 and 2, spacecraft that are on their way toward other worlds in this galaxy. This sample of Humpback song is in a section of the recording that includes greetings in 55 languages from 60 different countries.

Although Humpbacks are now part of the ambassadorial elite of Earth, no one actually knows how they and other baleen whales produce sound. Baleen whales have a larynx, but they have no vocal cords and their paired blowholes release no bubbles when they sing. A laryngeal source for the sound is not ruled out, but much more research must be done to determine how baleen whales make sound.

In toothed whales, sound production is complex, but it is better understood than sound production in baleen whales. The external blowhole of the toothed whale hides the "monkey lips," the internal soft tissue of the dual inner nasal passages. The monkey lips can pass air to generate sound, much like we can purse our lips to making squeaking and kissing sounds. One "monkey lip" can be open while the other is closed, creating a variety of different sounds. All the while, the external blowhole stays shut, so no air is released. The sounds made by toothed whales are primarily whistles, squeaks and clicks emitted in a variety of patterns.

Many groups of toothed whales have unique "dialects" different from other groups. All Orcas, for example, produce many similar sounds that are probably understandable from one whale to the next, but closer analysis reveals that one group will produce sound combinations that no other group does. Dolphins also have very sophisticated sounds and sound patterns. Many species have "signature whistles" for each individual, which are probably like human names. Signature whistles are often accompanied by a small string of bubbles released from the blowhole.

ECHOLOCATION

The use of echolocation, while it is rare in the animal kingdom, is not unique to whales. Bats and certain birds are also efficient echolocators, and there may be other animals that use echolocation that we are not aware of yet. Echolocation involves sending out high-frequency pulses or clicks and listening to how these sounds bounce off objects present in the vicinity.

Echolocation, particularly the underwater variety, is also known as sonar (*sound navigation and ranging*). Military organizations once applauded themselves for discovering and using such "advanced" technology. Some of this military pride was shattered upon learning that bats and whales had been doing it for millennia.

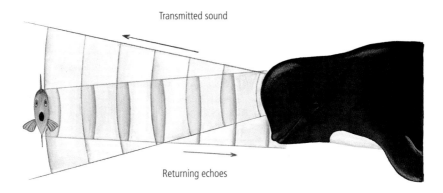

Transmitted sound

Returning echoes

As far as we know, only the toothed whales use echolocation. Some species, such as spotted dolphins, may even use such intense pulses that their prey is momentarily stunned, making feeding much easier.

When toothed whales emit the echolocation clicks, the sounds are passed through the melon—a specialized structure in their foreheads that focuses the sound. The melon is mainly low-density oil, and it gives toothed whales their distinctive, bulbous foreheads. When the outgoing signals hit an object, they bounce back in an altered form. These returning "echoes" are so detailed that the whale can perceive shape, size, texture, distance and probably many more features. The returning signals are received through the lower jaw, which helps transmit the sound to the modified ear.

Echolocation is not limited to surfaces. Evidence indicates that cetaceans can "see" inside things, even inside other bodies, to learn which females (human, dolphin or otherwise) are pregnant. Many interesting research projects involve dolphins and pregnant women, because the dolphins seem to be aware of the pregnancy and act differently around these women. The primary use for echolocation in whales, however, is for finding food and determining the immediate surroundings. The pulses are effective for at least 2500 ft (760 m), and they allow the whales to hunt even in totally dark or murky water.

MIGRATION

Both baleen and toothed whales may perform migrations of some sort. The baleen whales typically make long migrations between their feeding waters and their calving and mating waters. Most toothed whales, on the other hand, are more appropriately called nomadic, because their journeys follow food cycles rather than predetermined paths for certain activities. Sperm Whales, Bottlenosed Whales and Long-finned Pilot Whales make seasonal migrations, but in general, very little is known about toothed whale migrations.

In general, and in both hemispheres, baleen whales migrate from high-latitude feeding waters to low-latitude calving and mating waters. The whales often feed only in the high-latitude waters, and during periods of calving, mating and migrating, they consume little or no food. The foods that baleen whales feed on—primarily plankton, krill, copepods and small fish—are particularly abundant in the high-latitude waters. Some theories suggest the baleen whales migrate to warm waters each year because their calves may not be able to survive in the cold, food-rich water, but there is little evidence to support such claims.

The details of why whales migrate may forever remain a mystery to us, as may the mechanics of how they unerringly traverse thousands of miles of water. The long swim of a migrating baleen whale takes two or three months in each direction. It travels nearly constantly at speeds of just a few miles an hour. The cues a whale uses to navigate are not well understood. Perhaps it spy-hops occasionally to follow natural coastal features, or it may be able to detect subtle changes in water "tastes" and currents. Some researchers suggest that whales can use the sun and stars as a compass like we do, or they may be able to follow seafloor topography. Some cetaceans have the mineral magnetite (iron oxide) present in their bodies, and this is a key substance for biomagnetism. (Biomagnetism is when an animal can orient itself to the magnetic field of the Earth, and perhaps use this ability for traveling long distances.) Whichever way they do it, whales continue to dazzle the researchers with their ability to travel and properly navigate over long distances.

STRANDINGS

Strandings are staggering events where whales end up in shallow water and can no longer maneuver. If the tide goes out, the whale is left dry on the sand, where it usually dies. Stranding can happen to one whale or to hundreds of whales at a time.

No one seems to know why some cetaceans become stranded. Some people think that in areas of gently sloping beaches, the echolocation of the toothed whales is distorted. It is true that strandings occur more often with deep-water species, such as Sperm Whales or pilot whales, as if they become disoriented if they get too close to the coastline. Cetaceans that regularly live in coastal waters, such as dolphins and porpoises, rarely strand. In these cases, the individuals that strand are usually injured or diseased. Beluga Whales may strand when high numbers of them congregate into estuaries and shallow bays. As long as a Polar Bear does not find it, a stranded Beluga will live until the next tide comes to free it.

In situations where whales are found alive and stranded, do not attempt to touch them or help them. In some countries, it is illegal to help whales unless you have proper training. Unskilled "help" for a stranded whale has often resulted in greater harm to the whale and injuries to the person. The first thing to do in the event of a stranding is contact the nearest wildlife authorities or the police. If necessary, the immediate first aid for a stranded whale is to make sure its blowhole is unobstructed by sand or debris so it can breathe, and to keep its skin moist so it does not get sunburned or dehydrated.

DISPLAYS AND SURFACE BEHAVIOR

BREACHING: This behavior is a favorite for whale watchers. A breach is when some or all of the whale's body rises out of the water and splashes back in. Why whales breach is not clear. They may enjoy it, it may help rid the body of barnacles and parasites, or they may do it if they feel insecure or threatened. In some cases, whales breach repeatedly, much to the delight and astonishment of nearby whale watchers. Although many people assume that such instances are positive for both the people and the whale, some researchers suspect that the whale is breaching because of distress from boat harassment. Dolphins may breach in a high leap clear out of the water and spin or somersault while in the air.

LOB-TAILING: The lob-tail is when a whale forcefully slaps its flukes on the surface of the water while its upper body remains submerged. When a whale lob-tails, it can be interpreted in many ways. Some species are known to lob-tail as a sign of aggression, while others appear to do it for much more benign reasons, such as communication.

SPY-HOPPING: Most whales engage in spy-hopping, especially while traveling. Spy-hopping is when a whale raises its head almost vertically out of the water as if to get a better look around. This may be exactly what it is doing, because whales typically only rise until their eyes are exposed and no more.

FLIPPER-SLAPPING: Cetaceans may occasionally roll to one side and slap their flippers against the surface of the water. This behavior may be repeated several times in a row, but we do not understand what it signifies.

FLUKING: Before a whale dives, it frequently raises its flukes above the surface of the water. For many species, this action indicates that a long, deep dive has started. Many researchers use the markings and scars on the flukes of whales to identify and catalog individuals.\

LOGGING: For most species, one to several whales may "log" at the surface as a form of rest. When several individuals log, they all face the same direction and stay in a close group. Logging requires minimal effort, but is not an unconscious state, because the whale must remain at least semi-conscious at all times in order to breathe.

BOW-RIDING: Dolphins, porpoises and some small whales often engage in bow-riding and wake-riding. Dolphins appear to enjoy this activity, and people certainly enjoy watching them. The pressure wave created from a moving boat pushes the dolphins along at great speeds with minimal energy output by the animal.

RUBBING: Rubbing is a behavior done by several species and is probably to massage the skin, aid in molting or simply to feel good. Orcas massage themselves on shallow underwater beaches of rounded pebbles, which in some cases is visible to a boater above.

PLAYING: Probably all cetaceans engage in playing activity. Play can be anything, and may involve juveniles learning particular behaviors that will aid them as adults. If you see whales or dolphins playing at the surface, enjoy watching them, but try not to disturb their fun or harass them.

BLOWING: One of the first indications that a whale is nearby is the distinct blow it makes upon surfacing. The blow of a whale is probably made visible by a combination of factors. The difference in temperature between the whale's lungs and the outside air, some seawater from the skin's surface and accumulated droplets of mucus and oils from the whale's lungs and nasal passages probably all contribute to the blow. The shape and size of the blow vary between species. Some species, such as the Sperm Whale, have such unique blows that seeing the blow alone can identify the whale. Within a species, blow shape and size also vary. Typically, the first blow after a long dive is louder and bigger than successive blows. Side views of a blow may not be as distinct as views from the front or rear. The blows illustrated on the following pages are to scale and are all viewed from the front.

DIVE SEQUENCE: The most frequently observed activity at the surface is the dive sequence. Beginning with a blow, the dive sequence reveals certain characteristics about the animal. The shape of the head and the blowhole, the length of the back, the dorsal fin, any dorsal knuckles or bumps, the tail stock and the flukes are all features that may be seen in a dive and are often diagnostic enough to identify the species.

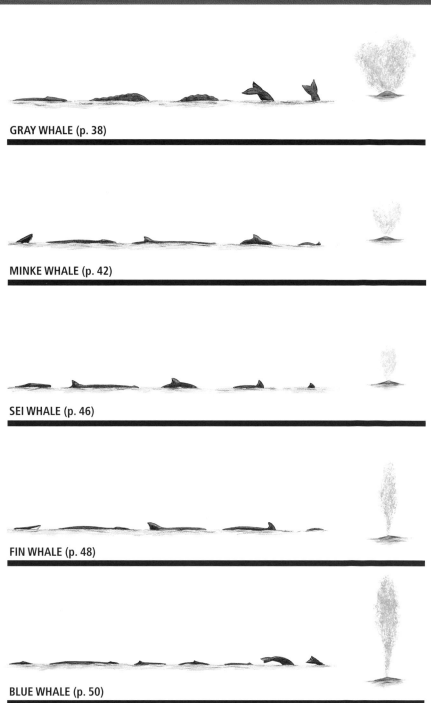

GRAY WHALE (p. 38)

MINKE WHALE (p. 42)

SEI WHALE (p. 46)

FIN WHALE (p. 48)

BLUE WHALE (p. 50)

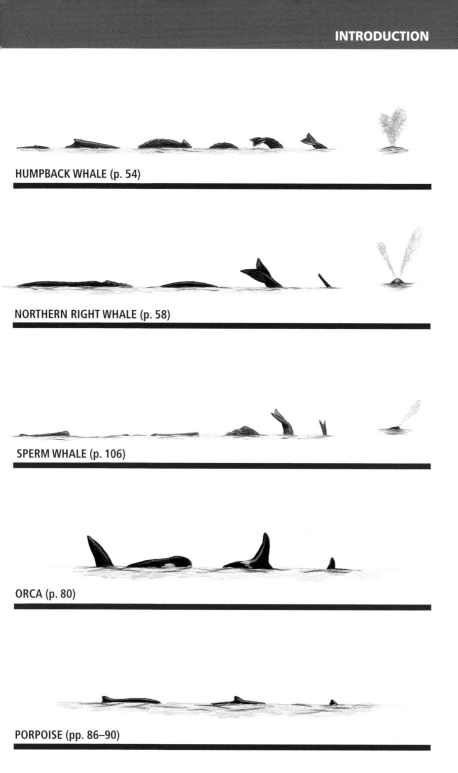

HUMPBACK WHALE (p. 54)

NORTHERN RIGHT WHALE (p. 58)

SPERM WHALE (p. 106)

ORCA (p. 80)

PORPOISE (pp. 86–90)

Intelligence and Whale Research

A common question people ask is "How intelligent are whales?" To answer honestly, we do not know. Many studies have been done with whales to determine their intellectual abilities, but we do not have accurate ways of measuring intelligence in animals other than humans. Also, whales, dolphins and porpoises differ in intelligence amongst themselves. For example, most people would agree that Orcas and Bottlenosed Dolphins are more intelligent than river dolphins. Even how we define intelligence is ambiguous: it can mean independent thinking, analytical skills, understanding and evaluation skills or the ability to use reason and judgment in daily life. Intelligence can also be measured as a correlation between brain size and brain complexity.

Another difficulty arises in how we test cetacean intelligence. We require whales and dolphins to learn our signals and sounds, and then complete performance and ability tests. The inherent flaw in these procedures is that we are not measuring how intelligent a whale is with such tests, we are only learning how well they do on tests designed by us. By learning the sounds, signals and performance abilities of whales and dolphins in their own environment, we may learn far more about the intelligence of these creatures.

Looking at the brain of a cetacean is an indication of its potential intelligence. Unfortunately, the ratio of body size to brain size (also called the encephalization quotient) does not directly correlate with intelligence level. Bottlenosed Dolphins have larger brains than humans in absolute terms, but their encephalization quotient is smaller. Bottlenosed Dolphins and chimpanzees have similar encephalization quotients. The complexity of a Bottlenosed Dolphin's brain is high, however, and it has well-developed cerebral cortices (the part of the brain associated with learning and abstract thought). Some people argue that this level of complexity serves to coordinate their motor processes and echolocation, rather than being a sign of true intelligence.

Problem solving and the ability to learn are two well-accepted ways to assess intelligence. Whales in the wild show signs of teaching each other new things they have learned, and certainly mothers teach their calves many techniques for living. In captivity, cetaceans learn complex routines very quickly, and they even learn our language symbols. Studies with Bottlenosed Dolphins indicate they understand some abstract concepts like "sameness" and "difference." Using sign language, a dolphin easily understands the difference between "take the ball to the hoop" and "take the hoop to the ball." Dolphins seem quite capable of learning the basics of our language and signals, but we have still a long way to go to learn their sounds and language. Researchers debate about definitions of language, and whether or not cetaceans have true language. Nevertheless, it is clear to any observer that dolphins use sounds between one another and these sounds appear to have intention and even meaning.

Some dolphins and whales appear to have good levels of problem solving, and there are several well-known examples of problem solving in wild cetaceans. In the wild, Bottlenosed Dolphins have been observed using tools in problem situations, such as wielding the spines from a dead, poisonous fish to oust an eel from its crevice. Many researchers believe that the cooperative bubble-netting demonstrated by Humpback Whales is an intentional act of cooperation to solve a common problem, although other researchers feel this behavior may be simply instinctive. During heavy whaling years two centuries ago, Sperm Whales were frequently reported to swim and dive in directions upwind when pursued by a sailing vessel. Because sailing vessels cannot travel directly upwind, this behavior could indicate a high level of reasoning or problem solving ability in Sperm Whales, as well as an awareness of the consequences of being caught.

The difficulty with problem solving studies is to differentiate between instinctual responses and actual judgment and evaluation. Problem solving and behavioral studies are excellent forms of research that continually lead to a greater understanding of cetacean ability.

In Washington, Oregon and neighboring regions, whale research in the wild is becoming much more sophisticated. Satellite transmitters are being attached to many species to better understand their migration patterns. Photographic catalogs are used to identify hundreds of individual whales of many different species, especially Orcas and Humpback Whales. Orcas are reliably identified by the shape and scarring of their dorsal fins and by the shape and coloration of the "saddle" patch directly behind the dorsal fin. Humpback Whales can be recognized by the undersides of their tail flukes. The fluke coloration, shape and scarring patterns are used to identify individuals just like fingerprints are used to identify humans. Knowing the individuals means we can follow their movements and record their behaviors with much greater detail.

New diving technology allows divers to breathe underwater without releasing bubbles. Because many whales release bubbles as a threat or when they are alarmed, a diver who releases bubbles likely disturbs the whale and therefore alters its behavior. Since researchers have used this new diving technology, they have been able to observe male Humpbacks as they "sing." With the old kind of scuba gear, the bubbles alerted the whale and it would immediately stop singing. The challenges of studying whales in the wild are great, but as we develop and apply new technology we are able to learn more about the whales and their environment.

Whale Lore:
From Legends to Modern Mythology

For many cultures, whales have been powerful symbols of creation, perfection and even prophecy. Perhaps the earliest depiction of a cetacean is found in Norway, where an ancient carving of an Orca lingers on the coastal rocks and is believed to be about 9000 years old. The ancient Greeks recognized the intelligence and friendliness of dolphins, and they regularly used dolphin motifs in their sculptures, frescos, pottery, coins and paintings. Certain accounts of Greek mythology attach great meaning and spirituality to the dolphin. In one version of creation, all of life originated within a dolphin, hence the Greek species name *delphys*, which means "womb."

On the northwest coast, many indigenous peoples included cetaceans in their mythology in some way. Whales, especially Orcas, are an important part of Native American tradition in northern Washington—they are meshed into the social, religious and imaginative life of the people. Because of the mythological importance of the Orca, this whale was never actively hunted by Native Americans.

A common myth about Orcas that permeates both literature and research is that Orcas have never attacked a human. Many Native Americans tell the story of Noht-sy-cla-nay, the man who created the Whale Killer (Orca). Noht-sy-cla-nay created this creature as a favor to the sea-lions, whom he stayed with for a time after his two evil brothers-in-law left him to die on a reef. Months later, after the Whale Killer was created, Noht-sy-cla-nay saw his brothers-in-law in a canoe, and he summoned his Whale Killer to smash the canoe and drown the men inside. After this revenge, Noht-sy-cla-nay said to the Whale Killer, "I made you to kill whales and help the sea-lions, so you must never kill another man again."

While the Orca was revered and protected from killing, other whales were valuable for their meat and oil. The Native Americans of the northwest coast believed that whales, dolphins and porpoises lived in underwater villages similar to those of humans. On occasion, the chief whale would order an individual to allow itself to be caught by humans, in order to give food to the people in need. In gratitude, these people would throw bones and intestines back into the water, in the belief that these remains would sink back to the whale's village and be renewed into another life.

In more recent centuries, many humans feared whales, and contact with them was limited either to hunting or to occasional events of strandings. Mariners told outlandish stories of attacks by great sea creatures that spouted a toxic substance capable of peeling away your skin and blinding your eyes. Artists engraved terrible scenes of freakish giants capsizing boats and lashing out with their tails. Such perceptions were later replaced by phrases like "gentle giants" and stories of whales and dolphins saving human lives. These stories may be true, but the value and appreciation of cetaceans is not dependent solely on their interaction with humans. Indeed, the truth about whales lies somewhere in-between: they are not quite the gentle and obsequious giants that many people believe them to be, but they are certainly not evil behemoths that lurk beneath our boats ready to strike.

Whale mythology is not limited to the historical perceptions and accounts of these great

Orca totem pole

creatures. Throughout modern literature and arts, whales have been exemplified, celebrated and somewhat idealized. Some famous works include Herman Melville's *Moby Dick*, Hollywood's *Star Trek: The Voyage Home* and *Free Willy*, television's *Flipper* and even Disney's *Pinocchio*. Such stories and films continually add to the rich tradition of whale lore.

Today, the perception and treatment of whales varies considerably between different people of the world. Many people view the whale as a superb opportunity to study mammalian adaptation, while others see the whale as a form of entertainment. Many societies hunt whales for meat and profit; others consider the whale a creature of inherent value outside human valuation schemes.

Regardless of how we look at whales, we share an increasingly intricate relationship with them. Whales, dolphins and porpoises now attract millions of people each year to coastal areas throughout the world. Their special intrigue comes of their intelligence and sheer magnificence. Watching a Humpback Whale breach and fall back into the water with a tremendous splash, or seeing a dolphin's eye turn to look at you as it bow-rides against your boat are extraordinary encounters that leave behind a feeling of contact with very special creatures. Cetaceans demand our respect as powerful creatures that can be very friendly and inquisitive in most circumstances, but rightfully protective and aggressive when they are harassed.

Whales in Peril

UNDERSTANDING WHALING

For centuries, whaling was considered a heroic profession that provided many necessary raw materials for a growing society. While the men were at sea, the needs of the people back on land perpetuated the demand for whale products. A staggering array of goods were made from whale parts, making a list so long and composing so many unexpected products that it is no wonder the whaling industry was lucrative.

Whale oil was used in lamps, lipsticks, soaps, shampoos, cooking goods, ice cream, crayons, glycerin for explosives, lotions, machinery lubricants, candles, leather processing, varnishes, adhesives—the list includes virtually everything that requires oil in some way. Baleen from whales has been used for only slightly fewer things, including, but not limited to, umbrella ribs, corsets, whips, window shutters, fishing rods, dress hoops, hairbrushes and shoehorns. Whale meat and blubber was—and still is—eaten by many people; teeth were used as ivory for artworks or piano keys; bones were used for building structures or were ground down to make fertilizer; tendons were used for string and catgut; whale skin could be tanned for leather and the intestinal linings could be stretched and used as transparent window panes. Even ambergris, a hard and waxy digestive by-product that forms in the gut of a Sperm Whale, was used as a fixative for perfumes and once valued at up to $806 a pound.

Most people who hunted whales made tremendous effort to utilize every part of the whale and leave nothing to waste. The major difference in usage between groups of people was that some cultures were subsistence whalers and required the whale for their survival, while other cultures were commercial whalers and used the whale for profit.

The evidence of a successful whaling industry is indisputable—millions of whales have been killed over the last two centuries, so many, in fact, that several species may never recover. In the 1940s, when whale populations were at their lowest, no one could deny that if whaling was not dramatically curtailed, there would be no more large whales. From sheer necessity, the International Whaling Commission (IWC) formed in 1948 and began the first management strategy for the industry and the countries involved in whaling. Unfortunately, the quotas and agreements developed by the IWC were never adhered to, and whaling continued. Moreover, for those countries that reported their annual whale takes to the IWC, most figures were as low as 5 percent of the actual number of whales that they killed. Even now, many countries still hunt whales for sustenance, and others still hunt whales for profit.

A strong argument can be made that the small reduction in whaling that occurred up until the early 1990s happened not because of a global effort to save the whales, but because of a combination of two circumstances: primarily, the whale populations were decimated and catches of hundreds of whales each month were no longer possible; secondarily, owing to the evolution of society, our demand for whale products also changed. Electricity greatly reduced the need for whale oil as a lighting agent, and plastics replaced many of the uses for baleen (and corsets, thankfully, went out of fashion).

Explosive harpoon

In view of the large number of uses for whale products, and though it may not be condonable, it is at the very least understandable that the industry heightened to the point of over-exploiting the resource. After 1925, the combined effect of explosive harpoons, high-speed whaling vessels and floating whale-processing factories marked the peak of commercial whaling. The catch sizes over the next few decades alone were staggering, especially in Antarctic waters. The Fin Whale, previously too fast for the whaling vessels to catch, took the brunt of the onslaught, and nearly 750,000 were killed. Other large whales were taken as well: more than 360,000 Blue Whales, 200,000 Humpback Whales, 200,000 Sei Whales, nearly 400,000 Sperm Whales and more than 100,000 Minke Whales. These numbers represent just a short period in whaling history when whaling vessels could finally catch the faster whales. In the 1800s, the numbers are equally high for the slower whales, such as the right whales and Bowhead Whale.

Only in the past 10 years has there been a real and obvious reduction in the number of whales killed annually. This change is attributable to the efforts of conservation groups and a worldwide awareness of the plight of whales. Unfortunately, many species are far from safe, and their numbers are far from stable. The Northern Right Whale is undeniably the most endangered large whale on Earth—only a few hundred survive, and most biologists fear it is too late for this species.

WHALING IN THE PACIFIC NORTHWEST

The history of whaling on the northwest coast is long and certainly diverse. The earliest whales hunted were the slow Northern Right and Gray whales. Putting a date on the first whaling event is nearly impossible, however, because people were known to eat small whales as early as 6000 years ago. Whether these whales were found stranded or were actually hunted is unknown. Almost certainly, Native Americans hunted whales 2000 years ago.

The Makah, Quinault and Quileute people of the Olympic Peninsula were probably among the region's earliest whalers. Makah whaling was controlled by a chief who had the spiritual power necessary to bring whales close to shore and enough skill and strength to kill them.

The method used by Makah whalers was unlike any other in the region. Makah hunters harpooned a whale and then attached numerous seal bladder floats to it. These floats prevented the whale from diving and soon tired the whale. As the whale lost its agility, the hunters in their canoes would herd the whale closer to shore. Eventually, the whale would be beached, or nearly so, and the hunters could finish their job.

Most Native American groups along the coasts of Washington and Oregon probably hunted whales or at least scavenged them at some time. For peoples other than the Makah, killing a whale occurred at sea and was only half the battle. Once the whale was dead, the people had to tow its enormous body back to shore behind their comparatively small canoes. Whaling on the northwest coast continued at this subsistence level for centuries, until widescale commercial whaling entered the region.

By the mid 1800s, European and American whalers were cruising the West Coast to hunt migrating whales. Shore-based industries were common along the entire West Coast, and each large factory was able to process up to 1000 or more whales in a year. Many of the American whaling companies established their factories in Alaska, or joined with Canadian companies to build factories in British Columbia. Bay City station and Gray's Harbor station, both in Washington, processed whales until 1925, when shore-based whaling declined because of dwindling whale populations. Whaling continued in the North Pacific until at least 1970, but most activity was aboard factory ships, which processed the whales while still at sea, and most ships were from countries other than the United States or Canada.

Today, many countries are still actively whaling, and some do so illegally. Fortunately, the numbers of whales taken annually are nowhere near historic records, but many cetacean species cannot tolerate more loses. Additionally, a few of the Native Americans are allowed to hunt limited numbers of whales. The Makah, for example, were recently permitted up to five whales per year. Farther north, some Native Americans in Alaska and British Columbia have been granted the same right or are in the process of receiving this permission.

ENVIRONMENTAL CONCERNS

To simply criticize whaling as ecologically unsound is to impose a modern awareness on an industry that historically was in great demand. The industry supported and initiated many advancements in society and technology, and even the expansion of the Industrial Revolution was facilitated by whale oil lubricants. Ironically, the whaling industry in the Pacific Northwest made extensive contributions to whale science, and it is this core of knowledge about whales that now helps us protect and understand them. We have made many efforts to save the great whales from further decline due to whaling, but other more subtle threats exist that may be as dangerous to whales as the harpoon.

A sad fact is that the oceans, which cover 70 percent of the planet, are being used as dumping grounds for a plethora of wastes and by-products produced by modern civilization. Far too many countries have intentionally and accidentally dumped harmful wastes into the oceans, believing that the water will somehow hide or deal with the garbage that no one else will accept. Unfortunately, the oceans are not capable of sanitizing or hiding the billions of tons of toxic waste, agricultural chemicals, crude oil and plastic debris that are carelessly dumped in, and these harmful substances are now affecting water quality and marine wildlife health around the world.

The magnitude of the problem is difficult to grasp. Many countries dump billions of tons of untreated wastewater into the oceans. There are approximately 65,000 chemicals that are commonly used in industry worldwide, and all of these may end up in the oceans in some form or another. Chemical wastes—including DDT, organochlorides and heavy metals—stay in the environment for a long time. High concentrations can cause death of animals immediately, while low concentrations accumulate in the animal's tissues. Whales that eat small fish or plankton with toxic or chemical waste in their bodies end up storing these harmful substances in their blubber. In the worst cases, dolphins that have died from chemical poisoning and washed up on shore are so laden with pollutants that they themselves are classified as toxic waste. Also, a female's milk, which is made from the body's fat reserves, can be so full of organochlorides that the newborn calf dies. This kind of poisoning of the ocean and marine creatures is extremely insidious and difficult to remedy. It is essential to the health of the oceans that people are educated about how harmful wastes can be, and how to prevent the discharge from occurring.

One kind of pollution for which every person is responsible is plastic bags. Discarded plastic bags float in the water column and so closely resemble jellyfish and squid that many whales gulp them down. Eventually, a whale's digestive system is so blocked by plastic bags that it dies of starvation. Originally, when creatures that eat jellyfish or squid—such as whales and sea turtles—were found dead on shore, the cause of their deaths was unknown. It was only after autopsies that plastic bags were found to be the problem. Millions, or maybe even billions, of plastic bags are discarded every day, many of which will end up floating in the oceans.

There is no easy answer to the problem of marine pollution. Of course, the careless discarding of harmful products into the water must be curtailed, but the existing pollution in the water is not so easily cleaned up.

Fishing nets are also responsible for the deaths of innumerable cetaceans each year. The purse-seine nets commonly used for fishing often catch small whales, dolphins and porpoises. Once caught in a net underwater, a cetacean drowns because it must breathe air. When the nets are pulled in, the bodies of the drowned cetaceans must be untangled from the net. Eventually, a net is so full of holes that it is irreparable, and it is often discarded into the water. These discarded "ghost" nets continue to catch sea creatures and small cetaceans while they float freely through the ocean. Eventually a ghost net sinks to the bottom from the weight of the bodies trapped in its mesh. Large whales may become entangled in ghost nets too, and they end up towing the net with them wherever they go. The net ultimately digs into the whale's flesh, causing life-threatening injuries and preventing it from feeding properly.

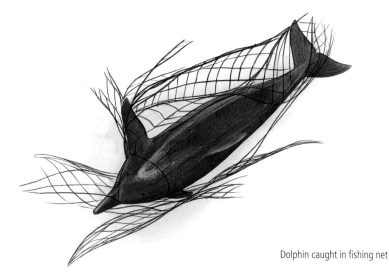

Dolphin caught in fishing net

If you are out whale watching and you see a whale entangled in a fishing net, the best course of action is to report this whale and its location to an emergency hotline. The telephone numbers and addresses of people who will help an entangled whale are available at the back of this book (p. 138).

Extreme Whales

A simple truth about cetaceans is that many of their characteristics are difficult for us to understand. Their size, their weight, their communication—much of what makes a whale a whale is unlike anything else we know. Typically, our efforts to understand whales involve compartmentalizing the information so that it is more manageable for us. We like to discuss large whales in terms of minimum and maximum lengths and weights, and we frequently discount reports of overly large whales as either myth or inaccurate reporting.

The framework in which we view whales, however, is not absolute. If the maximum length of a Blue Whale is reported by several authorities to be 100 ft (30 m), that does not preclude a whale of 105 ft (32 m), or more, from existing. In fact, there is much evidence to support the idea that large whales may keep getting slowly larger the older they get. Whalers of 100 and 200 years ago recorded enormous lengths for many whale species. Because whalers typically took the biggest whales (a simple choice to maximize profit for energy output), they would have also taken the oldest whales. Researchers commonly suggest that the reason we do not see such large specimens now is that the existing whales are comparatively young. Such a suggestion has to be based on the assumption that whales keep growing. Is this merely an assumption, or can it be proven scientifically?

LENGTH

Few animals demonstrate extended growth, but all that do share similar characteristics in their bone structure. For an animal to keep growing in length, the vertebral column must also be able to continue growing. Animals that stop growing soon after sexual maturity, such as humans, have vertebral columns that cannot grow anymore. On either side of each vertebra is a cap-like bone, called the epiphysis. While the animal is growing these "caps" are separated from the vertebra by a cartilaginous plate. For most mammals, after sexual maturity these "caps" fuse to the vertebra and growing (in length) stops. For large whales, such as the rorquals, this fusion is greatly delayed after sexual maturity and many older whales that are caught still have unfused epiphyses.

Given this evidence, it should not be surprising to find accounts of extremely large whales. For small whales, dolphins and porpoises, the epiphyses probably do fuse early and they have maximum lengths. In most cases, the measurements in this book indicate the maximum records for each species, as well as the average. This average is the most likely size of whale for each species that you will see while out whale watching. A truth about nature is that there are always exceptions. For example, the maximum length stated herein for the Humpback Whale is 62 ft (19 m). This figure represents a reasonable maximum for the species. However, a female Humpback was once captured in shallow waters near Bermuda that measured a staggering 88 ft (27 m). Exceptional whales do exist, and they remind us that our measurements and descriptions are only guides, not rules.

DIVING DEPTH

Other whale extremes are also well documented. For example, the depth to which Sperm Whales can dive, or the weights of the large rorqual, Bowhead and right whales are all subject to revision as we discover greater or more exceptional examples. Good science is about taking new information and shifting our framework to encompass it, rather than discounting evidence as mere calculation error or myth. The weight of large whales is very difficult to determine, but we can reasonably assume that the larger a whale specimen is, the more it is going to weigh. The maximum weights recorded in this book are from unusually large whales. The generally accepted average weight is also included, and this figure corresponds to the average length.

Sperm Whales were once thought to dive to a maximum depth of about 5000 ft (1500 m). We now accept that Sperm Whales can dive much deeper. One of the deepest records is from two Sperm Whale males that were killed upon surfacing from water that was 10,500 ft (3200 m) deep. They both had freshly eaten bottom-dwelling sharks in their stomachs, indicating that Sperm Whales can dive as deep as this. Perhaps there is no maximum: the Sperm Whale is perfectly adapted to handle the stress of deep diving, and the determining factor of the dive depth may be availability of food or time without oxygen.

LONGEVITY

Current research on Bowhead Whales has turned up startling evidence that these Arctic-dwelling whales may live for more than 200 years. Interest in Bowheads sparked when Inupiat hunters found old spearpoints and arrowheads buried deep in the flesh of a few individuals. Some of these stone points are dated at up to 200 years old, indicating the whale could be several years older than that. The traditional methods used by researchers to determine the age of a whale do not work on Bowhead Whales. A new method that studies the delicate layering in the lens of the eye is being employed to determine Bowhead ages. This method has shown several individuals at 150 years or more, and at least one at 215 years old. We do not know the maximum life span of a Bowhead Whale, and some researchers suggest that 215 may still be conservative. At more than 200 years old, Bowhead Whales are now considered some of the longest-lived creatures on Earth, together with Giant Tortoises (150 years old, with disputed records at up to 200 years old) and Giant Clams (up to 220 years old).

WHALES VS. DINOSAURS

It is a popular belief that whales are bigger than dinosaurs. Although whales can be accurately measured for length, weighing these beasts is nearly impossible. As for dinosaurs, measuring their length involves speculation and educated guessing. Many dinosaur species are known only from a few separate bones, and determining the length of a complete animal is sheer inference. To complicate matters, paleontologists keep turning up larger and larger specimens. No one even knows which species is the biggest dinosaur. Weighing a dinosaur is, of course, impossible and any given measurement is only theory.

Certain rules in biology make this guessing game easier. We know, for example, that a marine animal can generally have a greater body mass than a land animal, because the water helps support the weight. The conclusion is that Blue Whales—at up to 200 tons (181,400 kg)—win as the heaviest creatures, while certain dinosaurs are the longest creatures that ever lived. The longest dinosaurs known include the Supersaurus, at 100–130 ft (30–40 m), and both the Seismosaurus and recently discovered Argentinosaurus, at 110–160 ft (34–49 m).

hale Tales & Record Breakers

This section attempts to clarify some of the frequently asked questions about whales and whale extremes. Keep in mind, however, that these answers are not absolute. As we learn and discover more about the marine world, we have to continually update our record sheets.

HOW MANY DIFFERENT WHALES ARE IN THE WORLD?
There are currently 81 known species of whales, dolphins and porpoises.

WHAT IS THE LARGEST WHALE IN THE WORLD?
Blue Whale: maximum record 110 ft (34 m).

WHAT IS THE SMALLEST WHALE IN THE WORLD?
Franciscana (river dolphin): 4^1/$_2$–6 ft (1.4–1.8 m).

WHAT IS THE HEAVIEST WHALE IN THE WORLD?
Blue Whale: maximum record 200 tons (181,400 kg).

WHAT IS THE LONGEST-LIVED WHALE?
Bowhead Whale: more than 200 years.

WHAT IS A WHALE SHARK?
A Whale Shark is a shark, not a whale. The modifier "whale" is used because this shark is very big (up to 60 ft [18 m] long).

WHAT IS THE FASTEST WHALE IN THE WORLD?
Atlantic White-sided Dolphin: 32 knots (59 km/h).

WHAT IS THE DEEPEST-DIVING WHALE?
Sperm Whale: deepest record 10,000 ft (3050 m).

HOW LONG CAN WHALES HOLD THEIR BREATH?
Sperm Whale: confirmed record 2 hours 18 minutes.

HOW MUCH FOOD CAN A WHALE EAT IN ONE DAY?
Blue Whale: up to 8 tons (7300 kg).

WHAT IS THE LONGEST MIGRATION MADE BY A WHALE?
Gray Whale: round trip (one year) 12,400 mi (20,000 km).

WHAT IS THE LONGEST PREGNANCY FOR A WHALE?
Orca: 15 to 16 months.

WHAT IS THE RAREST WHALE IN THE WORLD?
Yangtze River Dolphin (China): fewer than 100 remaining.

WHAT IS THE LOUDEST SOUND MADE BY A WHALE?
Blue Whale: 188 decibels, measurable for at least 1500 mi (2400 km) underwater.

WHICH WHALE HAS THE MOST BALEEN PLATES (ON AVERAGE)?
Fin Whale: 360 plates.

WHICH WHALE HAS THE MOST TEETH?
Spinner Dolphin: 224.

WHICH WHALE HAS THE LONGEST TEETH?
Narwhal: a single tusk can reach 10 ft (3 m) long. One in 500 males have two tusks.

WHICH WHALE HAS THE LONGEST BALEEN?
Bowhead Whale: 14 ft (4.3 m). One disputed report of baleen measuring 19 ft (5.8 m) in
length.

Baleen Whales

GRAY WHALE FAMILY (ESCHRICHTIIDAE)

The Gray Whale, which is the sole member of this family, shares some characteristics with both right whales and rorquals: like a right whale, the Gray Whale has a heavy appearance and an arched mouth; like a rorqual, it has throat pleats (although fewer and less effective ones) that expand when food-rich water is drawn into the mouth. Overall, the Gray Whale is a mottled gray color, bespeckled with many patches of callosities and barnacles. The Gray Whale is believed to carry more parasites, such as barnacles and whale lice, than any other whale.

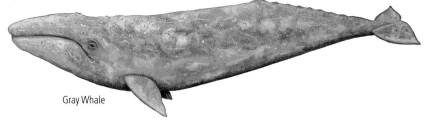

Gray Whale

RORQUAL FAMILY (BALAENOPTERIDAE)

The rorquals, numbering only a few species worldwide, include some of the largest whales on earth—the Blue Whale is reputed to be one of the largest animals that has ever lived. The name "rorqual" is derived from the Norwegian word *rorhval*, meaning "furrow," and refers to the pleats, or folds, in the skin of the throat. These throat pleats expand during feeding, allowing the throat to distend to an enormous, balloon-like shape when the whale gulps a massive volume of food-rich water into its mouth. The whale does not swallow the water; instead, the pleats contract and the tongue moves forward to push the water out through the baleen. Any crustaceans or fish are trapped inside the mouth to be swallowed whole. The only whales outside the rorqual family that have throat pleats are the Gray Whale and beaked whales, but their pleats are relatively few and have greatly reduced efficacy.

Fin Whale

There are six members in this family, five of which may be seen off the coast of Washington and Oregon. Rorquals are easily identified by their pointed snouts, flattened heads, long, slender bodies and relatively small dorsal fins, which are set about two-thirds of the way down the back. When a rorqual's mouth is open, the short baleen, which is continuous around the forward point of the jaw, is visible.

RIGHT WHALE FAMILY (BALAENIDAE)

This family includes two kinds of whales, the Bowhead Whale and the right whales. The Bowhead Whale is found only in Arctic and subarctic waters. Right whales have a much larger distribution.

The endangered right whales were once found throughout the world's cold and temperate oceans. Their total population now is probably only a few thousand individuals. There is much argument about whether there are one, two or even three species of right whales. Many scientists believe there is only one species worldwide, *Balaena glacialis*, while others feel strongly that this represents only the northern population, and that the Southern Hemisphere has a different species (*B. australis*).

Among the most distinct features of a right whale are the growths over its face and head. These callosities are masses of keratin topped with barnacles and teeming with whale lice. The whale lice may be pink, white, orange or yellow, and therefore give the callosities their unique color. The origin of these callosities is intriguing—they grow in all the places on the whale's head where a human would have hair. Specifically, they are found on the chin, the upper "lip," the top of the rostrum and above the eye. Keratin makes up both fingernails and hair in other mammals, and this may explain the origin of callosities in right whales.

Northern Right Whale

Gray Whale

Eschrichtius robustus

Gray Whales, which are among the most frequently observed whales, are famous for their extensive migrations. Almost the entire world population of Gray Whales travels back and forth between the cold Arctic seas where they spend summer and the warm Mexican waters where they spend winter, which amounts to about 12,400 mi (20,000 km) a year. A separate, small population of Gray Whales spends its summers in the Sea of Okhotsk off Siberia and migrates to the southern tip of Korea for winter.

During their summers in Arctic or near-Arctic seas, Gray Whales feed on amphipods, which are abundant bottom-dwelling crustaceans. These whales eat enormous quantities of food during their five to six months in the north to put on as much weight as possible. In migration, and especially during their stay in southern waters, they eat very little, and they may even fast completely. A Gray Whale can lose as much as 30 percent of its body weight between summers, and it is slim and hungry when it returns to the food-rich waters of the Arctic in early summer.

The Gray Whales' southward journey takes approximately three months: they leave the Arctic by late September and arrive in the waters off southern California and Mexico by late December. This migration coincides with the reproductive activity of the whales, and once in the warm waters, most females either mate or give birth.

By late February or March, Gray Whales begin their return to northern waters. Mothers with new calves may postpone their departure just a bit longer to ensure

DIVE SEQUENCE

38

RANGE: Gray Whales are now found only in the coastal waters of the North Pacific, primarily along the western coast of North America. A small population occurs along the eastern coast of Asia.

OTHER NAMES: Devilfish, Mussel-digger, Scrag Whale.

STATUS: Endangered (FWS); locally common in Pacific Northwest.

TOTAL LENGTH: up to 50 ft (15 m); average 45 ft (14 m).

TOTAL WEIGHT: up to 45 tons (41,000 kg); average 35 tons (32,000 kg).

BIRTH LENGTH: about 15 ft (4.6 m).

BIRTH WEIGHT: 1000 lb (450 kg).

that their young have the strength for the journey. The Gray Whales arrive in the Arctic again by May or June.

The Gray Whale, which once inhabited both the Atlantic and Pacific oceans, has been close to extinction at least twice in human history, and it now lives only in Pacific waters. The main reason for its decline was the whaling industry—the Gray Whale lives primarily in shallow waters, so it was an easy target. Aside from humans, the only predator of the Gray Whale is the Orca (p. 80), which might take young or weak individuals.

Now that Gray Whale populations are carefully protected, they are slowly recovering their numbers. The Gray Whale can be quite tolerant of humans, and it may even approach boats, which makes it a favorite of whale watchers throughout Washington and Oregon.

DESCRIPTION: The Gray Whale is easily distinguished from other whales by its mottled gray appearance and its narrow, triangular head. The head is slightly arched between the eye and the tip of the snout, and the jaw line usually has a similar arch. Like a rorqual, the Gray Whale has throat pleats—typically only two pleats, however, although three to seven are not uncommon. Over most of the body, but especially on the head, there are many yellow, orange or whitish patches of crusted barnacles or lice. The flippers, which are relatively small, are wide at the base but taper to a pointed tip. There is no dorsal fin, but there is a large bump where the dorsal fin should be and then a series of smaller bumps, or "knuckles," continuing along the dorsal ridge to the tail. The tail is distinctly notched and has pointed flukes. Female Gray Whales are generally larger than males.

BLOW: When viewed from the front or the rear, the Gray Whale's blow, which can be up to 15 ft (4.6 m) high, is bushy and heart-shaped. In some cases, the blow can look V-shaped. From the side view, the blow is bushy but not distinctive.

OTHER DISPLAYS: The Gray Whale actively partakes in breaching, spy-hopping and fluking. It will breach anywhere in its range, but most often in breeding lagoons in the south, often two or three times in a row. It rises nearly vertically out of the water and then comes down with an enormous splash. Spy-hopping is also common, and this whale may keep its head out of the water for 30 seconds or more. In shallow water, a Gray Whale may "cheat" and rest its flukes on the bottom so it can keep its head abovewater

uses its powerful tongue to push the silty water out through the baleen, trapping all the crustaceans inside. Most Gray Whales are "right-lipped"—as most humans are right-handed—and prefer to feed using the right side of the mouth. A close-up look at a Gray Whale's face will reveal its "handedness," because its preferred side will have numerous white scars and no barnacles. Inside the whale's mouth, the same uneven wear is visible in the baleen: on "right-lipped" whales, the baleen plates on the right side are more worn and shorter than the plates on the left.

REPRODUCTION: Gray Whales mate in December or January, and a single young is born $13^1/_2$ months later—in the following January or February. The young travel northward with their mother when they are only two months old, and they continue nursing until they are six to nine months old. Male Gray Whales are sexually mature when they are just over 36 ft (11 m) long; females are sexually mature when they are nearly 38 ft (12 m) long.

with minimal effort. Before a deep dive, this whale raises its flukes clear above the surface of the water. As it descends, the bumps along its dorsal ridge are visible, as are its distinctly notched tail and pointed flukes.

GROUP SIZE: Generally, this whale is seen in groups of only one to three individuals. It may migrate in groups of up to 15 individuals, and food-rich areas in the North Pacific can attract dozens or hundreds of Gray Whales at one time.

FEEDING: Unlike other baleen whales, the Gray Whale is primarily a bottom feeder. Its food consists of benthic amphipods and other bottom-dwelling invertebrates. A feeding Gray Whale dives down to the bottom and rolls onto one side, sticking out its lower lip and sucking in great volumes of food, water and muck. Once its mouth is full, it

Humpback Whale

SIMILAR SPECIES:
Humpback Whale (p. 54).

Minke Whale

Balaenoptera acutorostrata

The Minke Whale, the smallest of the rorquals, is a relatively common whale of the Pacific Northwest and Arctic seas. Despite its numbers, the Minke Whale is elusive and difficult to spot, because it spends less time at the surface than other whales— it usually takes only five to seven breaths before it goes under again. As well, the Minke Whale usually travels singly, and one little dorsal fin against an ocean of waves is easy to overlook. On the other hand, there are cases where a Minke Whale has surfaced right next to a boat, much to the surprise of the people aboard. Such occurrences are fleeting: the whale rapidly takes a breath and disappears as quickly as it came.

Several researchers who have studied Minke Whales consider them extremely intelligent and adaptable. Minke Whales are known to look for flocks of gulls, murres or auklets on the water—a flock of feeding birds advertises the whereabouts of a school of fish, making the fish an easy lunch for the whale. Although Minke Whales in central and southern oceans frequently use this tricky technique, the behavior is not as common in northern waters.

The study of the Minke Whale is still in its early stages, owing partly to the elusiveness of the animal, but also to its wide distribution. People wanting to study Gray Whales, for example, know exactly where to find Gray Whales, but Minke Whales can be

DIVE SEQUENCE

RANGE: The Minke Whale is found in every ocean of the world. In summer it is common in cold polar waters; in winter it migrates to more temperate waters.

OTHER NAMES: Piked Whale, Sharp-headed Finner, Little Finner, Lesser Finback, Lesser Rorqual.

STATUS: Locally common; insufficient data worldwide.

TOTAL LENGTH: up to 35 ft (11 m); average 27 ft (8.2 m).

TOTAL WEIGHT: up to 15 tons (14,000 kg); average 10 tons (9000 kg).

BIRTH LENGTH: 8–9 ft (2.4–2.7 m).

BIRTH WEIGHT: 770 lb (350 kg).

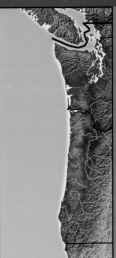

anywhere, and we have yet to determine their behavior patterns. It is known that many Minke Whales migrate between warm and cold waters each year, but some whales are believed to stay in one region year-round. The Minke Whale's winter mating and calving waters in the North Pacific remain a mystery. New advances in satellite technology and radio markers, however, may help answer some of these questions.

In the 1980s, the Minke Whale was the most heavily hunted baleen whale in the world. The populations of the larger whales had declined so dramatically by that time that whalers from many countries started to take this small rorqual instead. The Minke is still more heavily hunted than almost any other whale, but new regulations and international efforts have protected it in many parts of its range.

DESCRIPTION: The Minke Whale is a striking whale with whorls of white over its dark back and with white "epaulettes" on its flippers. On some individuals, the entire flipper may be white; on others, the white may be just a narrow band or even nonexistent. This variation in flipper markings is regionally specific, and it might indicate different subspecies. The coloration over the back varies considerably throughout the Minke's range: it can be dark slate gray, nearly black, deep bluish or dark brown. A Minke Whale's undersides are white or nearly white, and there are often swirls of white behind the flippers and again below the dorsal fin. This whale's overall appearance in the water is very sleek and streamlined. Its head is quite pointed, with a prominent splashguard before the blowhole and a distinct, single ridge to the snout. Relative to most other rorquals, a Minke Whale has a large, curved dorsal fin. Female Minke Whales are generally larger than males.

BLOW: The Minke Whale makes a small, quick, bushy blow that reaches a maximum height of about 9 ft (2.7 m). The blow may not

Flipper variations

FEEDING: Like the larger rorquals, the Minke Whale feeds mainly on krill, but it also eats some other invertebrates and small fish. It commonly lunge-feeds by swimming into a school of krill or small fish and gulping a large volume of food-filled water into its mouth. Its throat stretches like a big balloon, and as the whale closes its mouth and contracts the throat pleats, the water is forced out through the baleen. The organisms in the water are trapped in the mouth, and the whale uses its tongue to wipe the creatures off the baleen so it can swallow them.

REPRODUCTION: Minkes probably mate in late winter, but no calving waters have been found and very little is known about their reproductive cycle. The gestation period is 10 months. The nursing period is probably very short, because the calves are weaned before they arrive at the summer waters. Male Minke Whales are sexually mature when they reach about 23 ft (7 m) in length; females when they are 24 ft (7.3 m) long.

be visible, because it disperses quickly. On a very calm day, you may hear the blow rather than see it.

OTHER DISPLAYS: When a Minke Whale breaches, it comes far enough out of the water to expose its dorsal fin. The whale leaves the water at about a 45° angle, and it usually does not twist or turn as it comes down with a tremendous splash. This whale often arches back into the water headfirst, so the breach looks more like a dive than a belly flop.

GROUP SIZE: Minke Whales are seen either singly or in groups of two to four individuals. In areas of high food concentrations, a hundred or more Minke Whales may occur together.

Sei Whale

SIMILAR SPECIES: Sei Whale (p. 46); Fin Whale (p. 48).

Sei Whale

Balaenoptera borealis

DESCRIPTION: The Sei Whale is very similar to the larger Fin Whale (p. 48), and the two are hard to distinguish in the open ocean. The Sei Whale is mainly dark gray, blackish or bluish gray, with pale gray or whitish undersides, and it may have irregular, pale scars and marks along its body. Its baleen is finer and silkier than that of other rorquals, and its throat pleats are shorter. The dorsal fin is slender, upright and curved on the trailing edge. The flippers are dark on both sides, and they have pointed tips. The tail flukes are small relative to the size of the body. Female Sei Whales are generally larger than males.

OTHER DISPLAYS: Sei Whales breach infrequently, and rarely more than once at a time. They leave the water at a low angle and re-enter with a splash.

GROUP SIZE: Sei Whales are seen either singly or in groups of up to five individuals. Feeding waters attract larger numbers.

FEEDING: The Sei Whale feeds primarily on shoals or swarms of small fish or invertebrates, such as squid, krill and copepods. Its feeding style is similar to a right whale's: rather than lunge-feeding like the other rorquals, the Sei Whale skims steadily through food-rich water.

BLOW: The Sei Whale makes a blow that is similar to, but smaller than, those of the Blue and Fin whales. The blow is generally narrow, but not dense, and it may be up to 10 ft (3 m) tall. It is sometimes mildly heart-shaped.

DIVE SEQUENCE

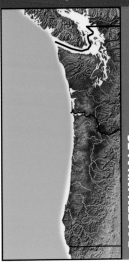

RANGE: Sei Whales are found in deep, temperate waters worldwide. In summer, they may feed in subpolar waters, but they usually occur in lower latitudes.

OTHER NAMES: Pollack Whale, Coalfish Whale, Sardine Whale, Japan Finner, Boreal Rorqual, Rudolphi's Rorqual.

STATUS: Endangered (FWS).

TOTAL LENGTH: up to 69 ft (21 m); average 48 ft (15 m).

TOTAL WEIGHT: average 35 tons (32,000 kg).

BIRTH LENGTH: 14–16 ft (4.3–4.9 m).

BIRTH WEIGHT: about 1600 lb (730 kg).

BALEEN WHALES

REPRODUCTION: Sei Whales mate and bear their young in mid-winter. The gestation period is 11½ months. The calves are born singly. These whales are sexually mature when they are about 95 percent of their total adult length.

Minke Whale

SIMILAR SPECIES: Minke Whale (p. 42); Fin Whale (p. 48); Blue Whale (p. 50).

Fin Whale

Balaenoptera physalus

DESCRIPTION: The unusual Fin Whale has a striking asymmetry of coloration on its head: the right side of the outer lower "lip" and the baleen on the right side are whitish, while the counterparts on the left side are gray. Oddly enough, the mouth cavity and tongue are gray on the right and white on the left. There is a distinct, pale gray, V-shaped mark behind the head. The overall body color is dark gray, silvery gray or brownish black, with white undersides. The dorsal fin is small and slanted backward. The flippers and flukes are dark on top and white below. There is a distinct ridge on the back from the dorsal fin to the flukes. Female Fin Whales are generally larger than males.

OTHER DISPLAYS: Fin Whales may make spectacular breaches, leaving the water at 45°, but they rarely show their dorsal fins. They may twist in the air as they come down with a thunderous splash.

GROUP SIZE: Fin Whales are occasionally found singly or in pairs, but typically in groups of 3 to 10 individuals.

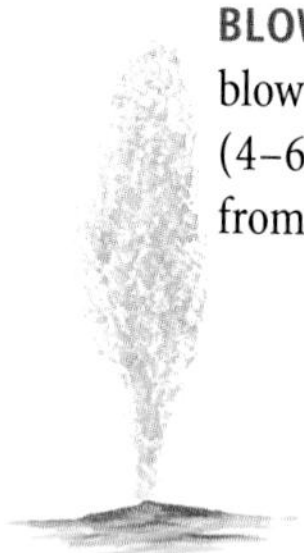

BLOW: The Fin Whale's narrow blow is quite dense and is 13–20 ft (4–6.1 m) high, making it visible from far away.

DIVE SEQUENCE

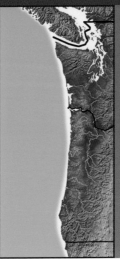

RANGE: Fin Whales are found worldwide in temperate and subpolar waters. They are more common in the Southern Hemisphere.

OTHER NAMES: Common Rorqual, Finback, Razorback, Herring Whale, Finner.

STATUS: Endangered (FWS).

TOTAL LENGTH: up to 89 ft (27 m); average 70 ft (21 m).

TOTAL WEIGHT: up to 140 tons (127,000 kg); average 80 tons (73,000 kg).

BIRTH LENGTH: 20–22 ft (6.1–6.7 m).

BIRTH WEIGHT: about 2 tons (1800 kg).

FEEDING: The main diet of the Fin Whale includes schooling fish, krill, squid, copepods and other invertebrates. Lunge-feeding is commonly seen, during which the whale often turns on its right side.

REPRODUCTION: Fin Whales mate in late winter. About 11 months later, a single calf is born. Males are sexually mature at 90 percent of their adult length; females at 75 to 80 percent.

Blue Whale

SIMILAR SPECIES: Blue Whale (p. 50); Sei Whale (p. 46).

Blue Whale

Balaenoptera musculus

Bigger than a dinosaur, bigger than a jet plane, bigger than three school buses—the words we use to describe the size of the Blue Whale hardly do justice to this leviathan. We cannot easily comprehend or describe how large the Blue Whale is, and perhaps this difficulty is reflected in the 18th-century humor used to name the species scientifically. As if in jest because any word we could use to describe this whale would fall short of capturing its true immensity, the Latin word *musculus*, meaning "little mouse," was used. The Blue Whale is so manifestly not a mouse that we can only smile at the comparison.

The Blue Whale is the most famous record-breaker in the animal kingdom. Not only is it the largest creature alive, and maybe the largest there ever has been, but it is also the loudest—its low-frequency pulses have been measured at up to 188 decibels. At birth, a Blue Whale calf is 23 ft (7 m) long, which is already larger than at least two-thirds of whales at their full adult length, even though the gestation period—about a year—is pretty typical of whales. The calf grows at an incredible rate: it puts on a staggering 200 lb (91 kg) a day, nursing 50 gal (190 *l*) of milk from its mother every 24 hours, and a weaned juvenile (about 1 1/2 years old) is about 50 ft (15 m) long. As adults, the largest individuals may eat up to 8 tons (7300 kg) of food a day during summer. Their hearts are as large as a car, and a small child could crawl through their arteries. A male's penis is about 10 ft (3 m) long.

Another record the Blue Whale holds, unfortunately, is that it is one of the most endangered large cetaceans on Earth. The height of the whaling industry in the late 1800s and early 1900s generated a relentless pursuit of Blue Whales. By 1950, the species was declared endangered.

DIVE SEQUENCE

RANGE: Blue Whales are usually found in open waters. Although their distribution appears to be worldwide, it is not continuous.

OTHER NAMES: Sulfur-bottom, Sibbald's Rorqual, Great Northern Rorqual.

STATUS: Endangered (FWS).

TOTAL LENGTH: up to 110 ft (34 m); average 85 ft (26 m).

TOTAL WEIGHT: up to 200 tons (181,000 kg); average 120 tons (109,000 kg).

BIRTH LENGTH: about 23 ft (7 m).

BIRTH WEIGHT: about 2½ tons (2300 kg).

In 1966, the International Whaling Commission gave a protected status to the Blue Whale, and it is slowly recovering. The total population is at least 6000, but there may be as many as 11,000 individuals.

The natural history of the Blue Whale is not well documented. Studies in the wild are difficult to undertake, and the bodies of stranded or hunted animals reveal limited information. In general, the Blue Whale migrates between low-latitude winter waters and high-latitude summer waters. Some populations, such as the one in the northern Indian Ocean, may reside year-round in the same place.

Three subspecies of the Blue Whale are known: the Blues in the Pacific Northwest belong to the subspecies *Balaenoptera musculus musculus*; the largest Blue Whales, *B. m. intermedia*, grow up to 110 ft (34 m) and are found in the Southern Hemisphere; the smallest, *B. m. brevicauda*, which grow to (only) 73 ft (22 m) and are often called Pygmy Blue Whales, occur in the tropical waters of the Southern Hemisphere.

DESCRIPTION: The enormous Blue Whale is typically deep slate blue or grayish in color, with variable pale gray or white mottling over the back. Its undersides are lighter, and range in color from pale blue gray to white to yellowish. A film of diatoms on the pale undersides results in yellowish bellies on some individuals and gives rise to the alternate name "sulfur-bottom." The Blue Whale has a broad, flattened head, a large splash-guard before the blowhole, and a pale throat with 55 to 88 pleats. The relatively tiny dorsal fin is located about three-quarters of the way down the body. The flippers are long, slender and darker above than below. The tail stock is very thick. The flukes are narrow, slightly notched and very wide—almost one-quarter of the body length. Female Blue Whales are generally larger than males.

side or belly. An adult's dive sequence is marked initially by the tall blow; then the whale's long back rolls over the surface. The dorsal fin appears well after the head has disappeared and the blow has dispersed. During its dive sequence, a Blue Whale may surface several times over a period of up to six minutes, and then it will dive for 10 to 20 minutes or longer.

GROUP SIZE: Blue Whales are typically seen in groups of one to five individuals, although good feeding waters can attract several more.

FEEDING: The Blue Whale specializes in eating krill—shrimp-like creatures that are about 2 in (5.1 cm) in length—and it rarely eats anything else. A Blue Whale usually rises up into a school of krill from below, gulping in hundreds of gallons of seawater. The water is squeezed out through the baleen either rapidly or over the course of several minutes.

REPRODUCTION: Gestation lasts 11 to 12 months for Blue Whales, and the peak calving period appears to be during winter, when the whales are at low latitudes. Calves are weaned when they are about eight months old. Both sexes reach sexual maturity when they are at least 80 percent of their adult length—about 10 years old.

BLOW: The blow of the Blue Whale is unmistakable: the narrow column of spray can rise at least 35 ft (11 m) high, and it can be seen even at a distance.

OTHER DISPLAYS: Not surprisingly, the Blue Whale is not acrobatic, although a juvenile may breach and make a tremendous splash as it falls back into the water, either on its

Fin Whale

SIMILAR SPECIES: Fin Whale (p. 48); Sei Whale (p. 46).

Humpback Whale

Megaptera novaeangliae

Humpback Whales are renowned for both their extensive migrations and their haunting songs. They are commonly seen by whale watchers, and they seem to enjoy performing for their boat-bound admirers. Other than brief bouts of fighting between males during the winter breeding season, Humpback Whales have gentle and docile natures.

One of the most famous places for viewing Humpbacks is the Pacific Northwest, where many of them spend their summers. When winter sets in, Humpback Whales migrate to the warm waters of either Hawaii or Mexico, and they may alternate their destination each year. As much as 5000 mi (8000 km) can lie between their high-latitude feeding waters and their tropical mating and calving waters. Humpbacks only feed during summer, and after their winter in the tropics they are slim and hungry.

The song of the Humpback Whale is one of the most impressive sounds in the animal kingdom. A Humpback can sing for a few minutes to half an hour, and an entire performance can go on for several days, with only short breaks between each song. The

DIVE SEQUENCE

RANGE: Humpback Whales are found throughout the world from polar to tropical waters. They migrate seasonally, so some regions have higher densities than others.

STATUS: Endangered (FWS); locally common in Pacific Northwest.

TOTAL LENGTH: up to 62 ft (19 m); average 45 ft (14 m).

TOTAL WEIGHT: up to 53 tons (48,000 kg); average 30 tons (27,000 kg).

BIRTH LENGTH: 13–16 ft (4–4.9 m).

BIRTH WEIGHT: 1–2 tons (900–1800 kg).

songs are composed of trills, whines, snores, wheezes and sighs, and when sung in a repeating pattern, the result is mysterious and hauntingly beautiful. While the true meaning of the Humpback's song eludes us, we do know that only the males sing and that they perform mainly during the breeding season. Many animals use sound to attract the opposite sex, which may be the primary function of the songs.

Male Humpbacks become very aggressive toward one another and battle to determine dominance on their winter breeding grounds. A dominant male becomes the escort to a female with a calf. Presumably, a female with a calf is one that is, or will soon be, receptive to mating.

DESCRIPTION: The Humpback Whale is slightly more robust in the body than other rorquals. The overall body color is either dark gray or dark slate blue, and the undersides may be the same color as the back or nearly white. The slender head bears many knobs and projections around the snout, and the mouth line arches downward to the eye. There are 12 to 36 pleats on the pale throat. The flippers are long and knobby and have a varying pattern of white markings. The tail flukes are strongly swept back and have irregular trailing edges. Like the flippers, the flukes have unique white markings that can identify individual whales. The dorsal fin can be small and stubby or high and curved, and several small knuckles are visible on the dorsal ridge between the fin and the tail. Humpbacks often host barnacles and whale lice. Female Humpbacks are generally larger than males.

Fluke variations

often inquisitive, and they may approach boats if boaters are non-harassing. When they breathe and dive, they roll through the water and show a strongly arched back. The tail flukes are lifted high only on deep dives.

GROUP SIZE: Humpbacks commonly live in small groups of two or three members, but some groups may have 15 members, and Humpbacks are occasionally seen singly. Good feeding and breeding waters usually draw large groups.

FEEDING: The Humpback Whale mainly feeds by lunge-feeding or bubble-netting, but much individual variation occurs in feeding styles. Its major foods are krill and schooling fish, such as herring, sand lance and capelin.

REPRODUCTION: The courtship behavior of Humpbacks is elaborate and involves lengthy bouts of singing by the males. Mating usually occurs in warm waters, and single calves are born following a gestation of about 11 1/2 months. The calves stay close to their mothers and nurse for about one year. Females reach sexual maturity when they are about 40 ft (12 m) long and males when they are at least 38 ft (12 m) long.

BLOW: The Humpback Whale makes a thick, orb-shaped blow that can reach up to 10 ft (3 m) high and is visible at a great distance. From directly in front or behind, the blow might appear slightly heart-shaped.

OTHER DISPLAYS: An acrobatic whale, the Humpback dazzles whale watchers with high breaches that finish in a tremendous splash. Other behaviors that it may repeat several times include lob-tailing, flipper-slapping and spy-hopping. Humpbacks are

Gray Whale

SIMILAR SPECIES: Gray Whale (p. 38).

Northern Right Whale

Balaena glacialis

This highly endangered animal was the most heavily pursued whale during the height of whaling. The name "right whale" is derived from mariners referring to it as the "right" whale to hunt: it is large, it has thick blubber and long baleen, and it swims slowly. The Northern Right Whale was the first whale to be hunted commercially, and hundreds of thousands of right whales were killed to feed the demand for whale oil and other whale products. By 1920, the Northern Right Whale was nearly extinct. There are still only about 200 right whales in the North Pacific and perhaps just 300 in the North Atlantic. In the Southern Hemisphere, the numbers are better—as many as 3000 Southern Right Whales (*Balaena australis*) still exist. The chances of seeing a Northern Right Whale along the West Coast are slim, but if such a sighting occurs and is confirmed, please make sure it is reported to the nearest marine research station.

When Northern Right Whales are seen in the wild, they can be quite approachable and inquisitive. Sometimes these whales are playful and bump and push floating objects in the water. As a cautionary note, these qualities of inquisitiveness and playfulness can result in a whale playing near or with your boat. Some kayakers have been surprised when their little boat was bumped or lifted in friendly jest.

As everyone knows, the greatest record-breaking animal in the world is the

DIVE SEQUENCE

RANGE: Northern Right Whales are found in polar and temperate waters of the Northern Hemisphere. They favor offshore waters rather than the open ocean.

OTHER NAMES: Black Right Whale, Biscayan Right Whale.

STATUS: Critically endangered (FWS).

TOTAL LENGTH: up to 60 ft (18 m); average 45 ft (14 m).

TOTAL WEIGHT: up to 95 tons (86,000 kg); average 60 tons (54,000 kg).

BIRTH LENGTH: 15–20 ft (4.6–6.1 m).

BIRTH WEIGHT: about 1 ton (910 kg).

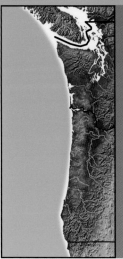

lue Whale (p. 50). The understated Northern Right Whale, however, wins a few titles of its own. While not a very noble title of recognition, the Northern Right Whale may well be the slowest whale on Earth. Less charitable still, it is one of the most robust (or fattest) whales, considering its weight per foot of body length. Its large tail is the broadest of all, relative to the length of the body. The one title this whale carries that may place it in the realm of nobility among cetaceans is for the largest testicles. With testes weighing in at 1 ton (910 kg), no other creature in the history of the world is as well-endowed. By comparison, the testes of the now-humbled Blue Whale weigh a mere 150 lb (68 kg).

DESCRIPTION: The robust Northern Right Whale is easy to distinguish because of the callosities on its head and its lack of a dorsal fin. Distinct callosities grow on the chin, on the rostrum, in front of the blowhole and above the eye. The body is nearly black, dark blue or dark brown, and it may show slight mottling or even patchy white spots on the belly. The mouth line is strongly arched upward and then drops nearly vertically to meet the eye. There is a distinct indent behind the blowhole and then a bulge continuing over the back. The baleen plates can be as long as 8 ft (2.4 m). The flippers are large and spatula-shaped, and they are dark on both sides. At close range, the finger bones in a flipper can be seen as distinct ridges. The flukes, also dark both above and below, are smooth, pointed and have a noticeable notch in the middle. Female Northern Right Whales are generally larger than males.

BLOW: When seen from the front or the rear, the right whale's distinctive blow is widely V-shaped. The sound is loud, and the spray can reach a height of 16 ft (4.9 m).

OTHER DISPLAYS: The Northern Right Whale is quite acrobatic considering its bulk. It often breaches, lob-tails, flipper-slaps and spy-hops. When it lob-tails, it may invert in the water to such a great extent that it appears to be doing a headstand.

hairs of the baleen plates and eventually swallowed. This whale skim-feeds wherever the food is present—at the surface or at depth.

REPRODUCTION: The Northern Right Whale has never managed to recover its numbers the way other whales have. The reasons are not clear, but the combination of isolated populations and a slow reproductive rate may be responsible. Females give birth only once every three or four years. Although these whales court and mate year-round, peak conception appears to be in winter, as is calving, which indicates a gestation period of about one year. Both sexes are sexually mature when they are 75 to 80 percent of the adult length.

GROUP SIZE: These right whales are typically found in small groups of two or three individuals. Sometimes a group numbering up to 12 members is seen. Seasonal feeding waters attract larger numbers of whales at certain times.

FEEDING: A remarkably efficient filter-feeder, the Northern Right Whale feeds on some of the smallest zooplankton in the sea. The primary food is tiny krill and other copepods. To feed, the whale swims slowly with its mouth open. The unique shape of the baleen makes the mouth look like a cave. As the whale progresses through a concentration of copepods, the water enters the "cave" and passes through the baleen. All of the creatures are trapped against the silky

Gray Whale

SIMILAR SPECIES: Gray Whale (p. 38).

Toothed Whales

OCEAN DOLPHIN FAMILY (DELPHINIDAE)

This large family of toothed whales represents the true ocean dolphins, and it includes some of the most well-known cetaceans—aquariums, movies and anecdotal accounts have made Bottlenosed Dolphins and Orcas world famous. There are at least 33 delphinid species worldwide, but some evidence indicates that certain species, like the Bottlenosed Dolphin, may actually be two or three distinct species. At least nine species of delphinids exist in the waters of Washington and Oregon.

Although many people call the Orca a whale, it is actually the largest dolphin in the world. The Orca and its smaller relatives, such as the False Killer Whale and pilot whales, are frequently referred to as "black-fish." Several authorities recognize these cetaceans as a separate family, but, based on anatomical similarities, they are best classified as delphinids.

Striped Dolphin

PORPOISE FAMILY (PHOCOENIDAE)

Porpoises, which number only six species worldwide, are widely distributed in the world, and there is very little range overlap between species. Although they superficially resemble dolphins, porpoises have unique features that set them apart from the better-known delphinids. They do not have a distinct beak, and their heads are quite rounded in appearance. Their body shape is a bit more robust than the streamlined dolphins, and their flippers are typically small and stubby. Unlike dolphins, which have conical teeth for holding and biting prey, porpoises have flattened, spade-shaped teeth that function to slice their prey.

Dall's Porpoise

BEAKED WHALE FAMILY (ZIPHIIDAE)

Beaked whales represent a large but poorly understood family of whales. They mainly inhabit deep ocean waters where people rarely visit, so accounts of their habits and behavior are few. Some species of beaked whales have never been seen alive and are known only from individuals found dead on the shore or pulled in by fishing nets. There are 20 known species, but unrecorded beaked whale species may exist in the vast areas of ocean that are still unexplored by humans.

The ziphiids are referred to as beaked whales because all of them have a prominent snout. Males have two or four teeth that erupt on their lower jaw, either in the front or along the sides. Females and juveniles usually do not have erupted teeth of any sort. The lower jaws of the males and mature females may slope upward in the middle, giving the appearance that the "lip" is wrapping around the upper jaw. The teeth of the males further exaggerate this arch, and in some species the two teeth wrap over the upper jaw. This feature greatly reduces the ability of the whale to open its jaws, but beaked whales are believed to feed by sucking their prey into their mouths. There are two V-shaped grooves on the throats of these whales.

Cuvier's Beaked Whale

DWARF SPERM WHALE FAMILY (KOGIIDAE)

The two whales in this family are the small, poorly understood cousins of the mighty Sperm Whale. Like the Sperm Whale, they live in deep water—they are only seen close to shore where the water depth increases rapidly—and very little information exists about their habits and natural history. Reliable sightings of these small whales have occurred in recent years, but most information is from a few stranded or caught individuals.

Dwarf Sperm Whale

SPERM WHALE FAMILY (PHYSETERIDAE)

The famous Sperm Whale, the subject of Herman Melville's book, *Moby Dick*, is the sole member of this family. Its most distinguishing feature is its extremely large head—the head of a male Sperm Whale may be as much as one-third of the length of its body. The exact function of the large head is still under much debate. Some people think its serves only to focus the echolocation clicks when the whale searches for food in very deep, dark water. Other theories suggest that the head, which is full of high-quality spermaceti oil, controls the buoyancy of the whale as it rises and dives through the water.

Sperm Whale

Striped Dolphin

Stenella coeruleoalba

DESCRIPTION: This streamlined dolphin is easy to recognize because of the distinct, thin stripe running from the eye to the underside of the tail stock. The Striped Dolphin is gray over most of its back, light gray on its sides and white or pinkish underneath. The border between the dark and light gray colors forms a zigzag below the dorsal fin. The dorsal fin is curved, and both the fin and flippers are dark on both sides. The pale gray flukes are slightly concave and notched in the middle. The beak is prominent and darkly colored.

BLOW: This dolphin does not have a visible blow, but if you are close enough, the sound of its breath is audible.

OTHER DISPLAYS: The Striped Dolphin is highly acrobatic, and it breaches the water to heights up to 23 ft (7 m). It may turn somersaults in the air or turn tail spins, re-entering the water in a graceful dive. This dolphin can "porpoise" through the water upside-down.

RANGE: Striped Dolphins can be found in warm-temperature, subtropical and tropical waters around the world.

STATUS: Locally common in some areas; insufficient data worldwide.

TOTAL LENGTH: up to 9 ft (2.7 m); average 7 ft (2.1 m).

TOTAL WEIGHT: up to 350 lb (160 kg); average 260 lb (120 kg).

BIRTH LENGTH: 3–3½ ft (91–107 cm).

BIRTH WEIGHT: unknown.

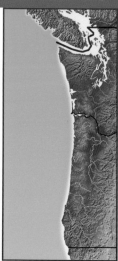

GROUP SIZE: Striped Dolphins are commonly found in herds of 100 to 500 members. In some circumstances, up to 3000 have been seen together.

FEEDING: This dolphin's primary diet is small to medium-sized fish and squid.

REPRODUCTION: Successful mating can occur in either summer or winter. After a gestation of 12 to 13 months, the female gives birth to one calf. Females are sexually mature at about 90 percent of their adult length. Males, although they are sexually mature when they are about 9 years old, are not socially mature enough to mate until they are 16 years old.

Short-beaked
Saddleback Dolphin

SIMILAR SPECIES: Saddleback Dolphins (p. 66); Pacific White-sided Dolphin (p. 70).

Saddleback Dolphins

Delphinus spp.

More so than any other dolphins, the saddleback dolphins confound both taxonomists and biologists alike. At least 20 species have been proposed worldwide, as well as several subspecies. Officially, the group was recently split into two species: the Short-beaked Saddleback Dolphin (*Delphinus delphis*) and the Long-beaked Saddleback Dolphin (*D. capensis*). As the names suggest, the latter has a longer beak than the former, and, in general, the Long-beaked Saddleback Dolphin has a longer and slightly slimmer body, more muted coloration and a thicker dark line from the lower jaw to the flipper than the Short-beaked Saddleback Dolphin.

These key differences are often insufficient for an accurate identification, however, because there are many color and shape variations within each species. Even the sexes vary slightly in color and pattern. Because these two dolphins are so difficult to distinguish in the wild, and considering their lengthy names, many people simply refer to them collectively as "saddleback dolphins." These two dolphins have such similar life histories and ranges that we have discussed them together here.

Like many other dolphins, saddleback dolphins are able to make an array of different sounds: they click, squeak and whistle, and they have a particularly high-pitched squeal that can even be heard from above the water. When large groups of saddleback dolphins are playing, they can be so loud and loquacious that they are heard long before they are seen. If the herd is startled, they bunch tightly together for safety.

Short-beaked Saddleback Dolphin

RANGE: Saddleback dolphins are widely distributed in warm-temperate, subtropical and tropical waters of the world. In the Pacific Northwest, they are not likely to be found farther north than the southern tip of Vancouver Island.

OTHER NAMES: Common Dolphin, Criss-cross Dolphin.

STATUS: Common.

TOTAL LENGTH: up to 8½ ft (2.6 m); average 6½ ft (2 m).

TOTAL WEIGHT: up to 300 lb (140 kg); average 170 lb (77 kg).

BIRTH LENGTH: about 2½ ft (76 cm).

BIRTH WEIGHT: unknown.

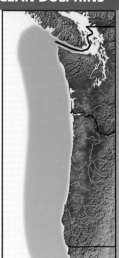

Saddleback dolphins are very wary of Orcas (p. 80) and sharks, and if the alarm is called they may retreat to lagoons or rough surf zones to avoid predators. Even when they are resting, they are alert for danger. Dolphins literally have the ability to sleep in halves: they are able to rest one eye while the other stays alert. Their brain also rests one hemisphere at a time, allowing for a constant state of awareness.

Unfortunately, one danger to which dolphins are oblivious is fishing nets, and a significant number of saddleback dolphins are killed each year by fishing activities. Saddleback dolphins may be at greater risk of getting caught in nets than other dolphins, because in some waters they associate closely with yellowfin tuna.

DESCRIPTION: This small to mid-sized dolphin is easy to identify because of its unique coloration. On its sides, beginning behind the eye, there is an arching, tan-colored patch. This patch can be quite yellowish or sometimes a dull muddy gray color. The tail stock is colored light gray, also in an arch, and where the gray meets the yellowish patch on the side, there is a distinct criss-crossing pattern. The back is mainly dark brown or bluish black, and the undersides are whitish. The beak is darkly colored and sometimes white-tipped, and there are streaks of white or gray around the face. A dark circle always surrounds the eye, and a dark streak runs from the lower jaw to the flipper. The broad flippers are dark on both sides, as are the pointed flukes. The triangular dorsal fin is centrally located, and often the center is lighter gray than the rim. The flippers, dorsal fin and flukes all trail backward, giving the dolphin a streamlined appearance.

Long-beaked
Saddleback Dolphin

Short-beaked
Saddleback Dolphin

of saddleback dolphins may be in the millions. Some groups as large as 2000 have been seen in warm waters, but a more typical group size is 10 to 500.

FEEDING: Saddleback dolphins feed mainly on small schooling fish, such as herring, anchovies and sardines. A group of dolphins typically herds the fish into a tight ball and then begins feeding. Such cooperative strategies are used by many species of dolphins. Feeding seabirds can attract dolphins to an area, because their flock usually indicates a sizable school of fish. Conversely, feeding dolphins can attract seabirds that benefit from the herded fish.

REPRODUCTION: The reproductive ages and lengths of saddleback dolphins can vary between different regions and sub-species, but generally females are sexually mature when they are 6 ft (1.8 m) long, and males when they are 6¹/₂ ft (2 m) long. Mating and calving can occur at any time of the year, and gestation is 11 to 12 months. The social structure of a group might influence courtship and mating.

BLOW: The blow of a saddleback dolphin is generally not visible. At close range, however, the sound of its breathing can be heard when it is in mid-leap.

OTHER DISPLAYS: Saddleback dolphins are exceptional acrobats, and they frolic and play in noisy displays. They may leap high out of the water and fall gracefully back in with little splash. They frequently bow-ride, and other displays include flipper slaps, chin slaps, lob-tailing and somersaults while breaching.

GROUP SIZE: Perhaps the most numerous dolphins in the world, the world population

Striped Dolphin

SIMILAR SPECIES: Striped Dolphin (p. 64); Pacific White-sided Dolphin (p. 70).

Pacific White-sided Dolphin

Lagenorhynchus obliquidens

Acrobatic Pacific White-sided Dolphins are favorites of whale watchers in the Pacific Northwest. These boisterous dolphins are so inquisitive and entertaining that they frequently "steal the show" from larger, less-engaging cetaceans. Do these dolphins enjoy entertaining? It would seem so, because they often increase their antics when boats full of eager whale watchers are around. On one occasion, to the astonishment of the viewers, an overly zealous individual leaped more than 10 ft (3 m) out of the water and accidentally landed on the deck of a large research boat. Of course, the exhibitionist was quickly returned to the water by the researchers, but the event remains a tribute to the impressive antics of these dolphins.

Pacific White-sided Dolphins and other members of the same genus are often referred to as "lags," a diminutive of their scientific name. As a group, these dolphins are not only acrobatic but very sociable as well. Together they surf ocean waves, catch wakes, ride bow waves and "porpoise" in unison. Sometimes, gatherings of 1000 or 2000 white-sided dolphins occur in offshore waters.

They also socialize with other dolphins and marine mammals, most notably the Northern Right Whale Dolphin (p. 84), seals and sea-lions.

Despite their gentle faces and social behavior, Pacific White-sided Dolphins can sometimes be pesky to larger whales, much like crows and magpies can be bothersome to your pet dog. White-sided dolphins have been seen clustering around the heads of Orcas (p. 80) and Humpbacks (p. 54) until the large whales get fed up and dive deep to get away.

RANGE: Pacific White-sided Dolphins are found only in the northern portion of the Pacific Ocean.

OTHER NAMES: Lag, Pacific Striped Dolphin, White-striped Dolphin, Hook-finned Dolphin.

STATUS: Common.

TOTAL LENGTH: up to 8 ft (2.4 m); average 7 ft (2.1 m).

TOTAL WEIGHT: up to 400 lb (180 kg); average 210 lb (95 kg).

BIRTH LENGTH: about 3 ft (91 cm).

BIRTH WEIGHT: about 30 lb (14 kg).

Sometimes they can even be aggressive, both with other species of marine mammals and with each other.

Recently, the numbers of these dolphins have been increasing in coastal waters, particularly in the straits and sounds of northern Washington. No one can accurately explain this occurrence, because the species was previously thought to prefer the open ocean. Many researchers suggest that these dolphins are simply following food availability.

Like most dolphins, Pacific White-sided Dolphins have acute senses that enable them to perceive their marine environment in an extremely sophisticated manner. Their sense of touch is many times greater than our own, and they can feel subtle changes in the pressure of the water around them. If another creature approaches a dolphin from behind its field of vision, the dolphin can detect the animal's approach from the pressure wave the animal displaces before it is seen or touched. This ability is undoubtedly

advantageous at night and in deep water where light cannot penetrate.

Because their senses of touch and echolocation are so highly sophisticated, it is a common misconception that dolphins have poor eyesight. In fact, dolphins have exceptionally good eyesight both in and out of the water. When a dolphin leaps into the air, it is able to see all of its surroundings. A human, by comparison, is faced with blurry images if they take their goggles off in water—a medium that is about 800 times denser than air.

DESCRIPTION: The Pacific White-sided Dolphin has a distinct and beautiful color pattern of white, gray and nearly black. Its back is mainly dark, and beginning in front of the eye there is a large grayish patch that extends down the sides to below the dorsal fin. Along the sides of the tail stock there is another similarly colored patch that may thin into a streak that runs forward of the dorsal fin. A distinct, dark lateral line borders the pure white undersides. The eyes are dark, as is the tip of its barely discernible beak. The most distinguishing feature is the

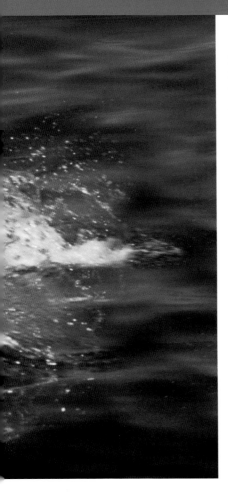

including dazzling breaches and somersaults. They often swim under the surface with just their dorsal fin exposed to slice and spray through the water.

GROUP SIZE: The Pacific White-sided Dolphin is commonly seen in groups of 10 to 50 members. Larger groups may sometimes form temporarily.

FEEDING: White-sided dolphins eat a variety of creatures, such as squid, anchovies, hake and other small fish. They feed in groups to better herd the fish, and each adult consumes about 20 lb (9 kg) a day.

REPRODUCTION: Calving and mating occur from late spring to fall, and gestation is estimated at 9 to 12 months. A mother nurses her calf for up to 18 months, and soon after weaning the female gives birth again. Both sexes reach sexual maturity when they are about 6 ft (1.8 m) long. Social maturity influences the age of first mating.

rearward-pointing, bicolored dorsal fin, which is dark on the leading edge and pale gray on the trailing edge. The flippers may be similarly colored, but they are often dark all over. The flukes are pointed, slightly notched and dark on both sides.

BLOW: White-sided dolphins do not make a distinct blow, but they often splash about and produce sprays that resemble a blow.

OTHER DISPLAYS: These acrobats perform virtually every kind of abovewater display,

Striped Dolphin

SIMILAR SPECIES: Striped Dolphin (p. 64); Saddleback Dolphins (p. 66); Harbor Porpoise (p. 86); Dall's Porpoise (p. 90).

Risso's Dolphin

Grampus griseus

DESCRIPTION: Unlike almost every other dolphin or whale in the world, the Risso's Dolphin becomes so heavily scarred that old individuals can appear almost white. The scars result either from teeth scratches incurred during sparring matches with each other or from squid bites. This dolphin is stout bodied and blunt headed. It has an unmistakably tall dorsal fin, long, sickle-shaped flippers and pointed, trailing flukes. Male Risso's Dolphins are generally larger than females.

BLOW: The Risso's Dolphin does not make a visible blow, but the sound of its breath is audible if the animal is close.

OTHER DISPLAYS: These dolphins are not as acrobatic as the smaller dolphins, but young animals may breach fully out of the water. They are also seen flipper-slapping, lob-tailing and spy-hopping. Although Risso's Dolphins rarely bow-ride, they often surf in waves and wakes.

GROUP SIZE: Risso's Dolphins are regularly seen in groups of 3 to 50 individuals. Some groups can be as large as 150, and good feeding areas can attracted several hundred dolphins at one time.

FEEDING: In deep water, these agile dolphins feed primarily on squid, although some medium-sized fish are also eaten.

RANGE: Risso's Dolphins are found in deep, tropical and warm-temperate waters throughout the world. They avoid cold polar waters.

STATUS: Common.

TOTAL LENGTH: up to 13 ft (4 m); average 10 ft (3 m).

TOTAL WEIGHT: up to 1100 lb (500 kg); average 880 lb (400 kg).

BIRTH LENGTH: 4–5½ ft (1.2–1.7 m).

BIRTH WEIGHT: unknown.

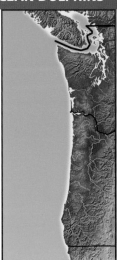

REPRODUCTION: Mating occurs primarily in spring, although the exact timing varies between different populations. Females give birth to one calf, usually in summer, after a gestation of 13 to 14 months. Both sexes are sexually mature when they are about 8½ ft (2.6 m) long.

Short-finned Pilot Whale

SIMILAR SPECIES: Short-finned Pilot Whale (p. 78); Dwarf Sperm Whale (p. 104).

False Killer Whale

Pseudorca crassidens

DESCRIPTION: The False Killer Whale is almost entirely black or deep gray, except for a light gray "W" or anchor-shaped patch on its undersides between the flippers. The snout is blunt and rounded, with the upper jaw protruding past the lower jaw. It has up to 24 teeth in each upper and lower jaw. The dorsal fin is upright, slightly rounded and located in the center of the dorsal line. The flippers appear slightly S-shaped because of the humped leading edge. The tail flukes are mildly pointed and notched in the middle. Male False Killer Whales are generally larger than females.

BLOW: Like most small whales, False Killer Whales make no visible blow.

OTHER DISPLAYS: When these whales surface, they often rise, or "porpoise," out of the water, exposing their flippers. Occasionally, they have their mouths open and show their teeth. False Killer Whales breach frequently and twist back into the water with a tremendous splash. They also bow-ride, wake-ride and even make acrobatic leaps clear out of the water.

GROUP SIZE: False Killer Whales are commonly seen in groups of 10 to 50 individuals. Gatherings of several hundred may occur throughout the year.

FEEDING: These fast whales feed mainly on squid and large fish, such as yellowfin tuna. They have been known to attack and kill other cetaceans, such as dolphins and even a Humpback Whale (p. 54).

RANGE: The False Killer Whale is found in the open ocean in tropical and warm-temperate waters. Some wanderers have been recorded as far north as Alaska.

OTHER NAMES: Pseudorca, False Pilot Whale, Blackfish.

STATUS: Rare.

TOTAL LENGTH: up to 20 ft (6.1 m); average 17 ft (5.2 m).

TOTAL WEIGHT: up to 2.2 tons (2,000 kg); average 1.6 tons (1500 kg).

BIRTH LENGTH: 5–6½ ft (1.5–2 m).

BIRTH WEIGHT: 180 lb (82 kg).

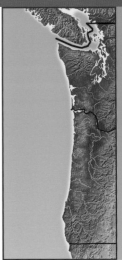

Short-finned Pilot Whale

REPRODUCTION: False Killer Whales mate successfully throughout the year. The gestation period is believed to be between 12 and 16 months. Males and females mature at roughly 80 percent of their adult body length.

SIMILAR SPECIES: Short-finned Pilot Whale (p. 78); Orca (p. 80).

Short-finned Pilot Whale

Globicephala macrorhynchus

DESCRIPTION: The Short-finned Pilot Whale is a small, black or dark gray whale. It has a bulbous head and an upward-slanting mouth, and some individuals have a light gray streak rising diagonally behind the eye. The dorsal fin is variable in shape, but it is usually arched strongly backward, with a rounded tip and a concave trailing edge. This whale has a light W-shaped patch on its underside between its flippers (see p. 76) and a light gray, oval patch on the underside forward of the tail stock. The flippers are pointed and strongly arched backward, and they are 14 to 19 percent of the body length. The flukes are also strongly pointed and notched in the middle. Short-finned Pilot Whales found in the Northern Hemisphere are typically larger than those in the Southern Hemisphere, and males are much larger than females.

BLOW: This whale makes a strong blow that is visible in calm weather.

OTHER DISPLAYS: The most commonly seen behavior of the Short-finned Pilot Whale is "logging," in which entire pods loll at the surface and are approachable by boats. This pilot whale rarely breaches, but it may be seen "porpoising," lob-tailing and spy-hopping.

GROUP SIZE: The typical group size is 10 to 30 individuals, although certain circumstances may attract several hundred pilot whales to one place.

FEEDING: The favorite foods of this whale are squid and octopus, although some large fish may be eaten.

RANGE: The Short-finned Pilot Whale is found in the open ocean in tropical and warm temperate waters. Some individuals have been recorded as far north as Alaska.

OTHER NAMES: Pothead Whale, Pacific Pilot Whale, Blackfish.

STATUS: Common.

TOTAL LENGTH: up to 23 ft (7 m); average 19 ft (5.8 m).

TOTAL WEIGHT: up to 4 tons (3600 kg); average 2½ tons (2300 kg).

BIRTH LENGTH: 4½–6 ft (1.4–1.8 m).

BIRTH WEIGHT: 140 lb (64 kg).

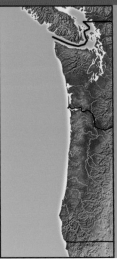

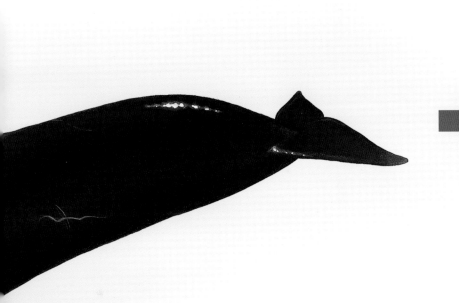

REPRODUCTION: Length at sexually maturity varies greatly, but for females the range is 11–13 ft (3.4–4 m) and for males it is 14–18 ft (4.3–5.5 m). The timing of mating varies regionally, and it probably occurs throughout the year. Gestation is roughly 15 months, and females nurse their calves for nearly two years.

False Killer Whale

SIMILAR SPECIES: Risso's Dolphin (p. 74); False Killer Whale (p. 76).

Orca

Orcinus orca

The Orca, with its striking colors and intelligent eyes, has fascinated humans for centuries. Once revered by the indigenous peoples of North America, the Orca is now an icon for such things as biodiversity protection and contact with non-human intelligence. Images of this white-and-black giant can be found on everything from coffee cups to international conservation documents.

The Orca lives in every ocean of the world, from the cold polar seas to the warm equatorial waters, and it is one of the most widely distributed mammals on earth. Uncontested as the top predator in the oceans, the Orca feeds on a wider variety of creatures than any other whale. It is regarded as an intelligent yet fearsome creature—it is the lion that rules the seas.

Studies along the Pacific coast of North America indicate that there are three distinct forms of Orcas. The two more common groups are the "transients" and the "residents," and they are distinguishable by appearance and behavior. Transient Orcas tend to be larger than residents, and they have taller, straighter dorsal fins. The transients live in smaller pods, from one to seven individuals, and they have large home ranges, whereas resident Orcas have small ranges and travel along predictable routes. Transients are more likely to feed on other sea mammals, they dive for up to 15 minutes,

Male

RANGE: The most widespread of all whales, Orcas are found in all oceans and seas.

OTHER NAMES: Killer Whale.

STATUS: Vulnerable; locally stable in Pacific Northwest.

TOTAL LENGTH: up to 32 ft (9.8 m); average 28 ft (8.5 m).

TOTAL WEIGHT: up to 11 tons (10,000 kg); average 7½ tons (6800 kg).

BIRTH LENGTH: 6–8 ft (1.8–2.4 m).

BIRTH WEIGHT: about 400 lb (180 kg).

they make erratic direction changes while traveling, and they do not vocalize as much as residents. Resident Orcas, on the other hand, feed mainly on fish, they are highly vocal, and they rarely dive for longer than three or four minutes.

Recently, a new class of Orcas has been identified. These "offshore" Orcas resemble the residents in appearance, but they usually live farther out at sea. Much more research is needed to accurately describe the offshore Orcas.

Unlike the rorqual whales, Orcas have never been hunted heavily by humans. Some hunting has occurred in the past several decades, but it has not threatened the total population. One form of hunting that has

taken many Orcas and their close cousins, the Bottlenosed Dolphins, is live hunting, in which Orcas are taken from the wild and introduced into the world aquarium trade, where they are expected to learn and perform tricks for the public. These activities cause much controversy, mainly because many people think that cetaceans are extremely intelligent animals and that keeping them in a closed aquarium is unjust. Much of what we have learned about cetacean intelligence and biology comes from studies of captive animals, and this knowledge can help us better understand and protect whales in the wild.

DESCRIPTION: The Orca is unmistakable: its body is black, its undersides and lower jaw are white, there are white patches behind the eyes and on its sides, its large flippers are paddle-shaped, and its dorsal fin is tall and triangular. The shape and size of the dorsal fin varies between each whale and can be used by scientists and whale watchers to identify specific individuals. Each whale has a uniquely shaped dorsal fin, which often bears scars, and a uniquely shaped saddle patch. Old males may have fins as tall as 6 ft (1.8 m), and the fins of some old individuals may be wavy when

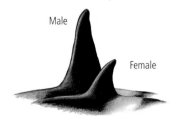

Male

Female

the water, lob-tailing, flipper-slapping, logging and spy-hopping. They may speed-swim, or "porpoise," with their entire body leaving the water at each breath. Subsurface beaches of rounded pebbles can attract many Orcas, which seem to enjoy rubbing their bodies on the smooth stones.

GROUP SIZE: Orcas travel in pods of 3 to 25 individuals. Some social gatherings may attract several pods at one time.

FEEDING: Orcas feed on a wider variety of animals than any other whale, partly because of their global distribution. Several hundred animal species are potential prey to these top predators of the sea, including, but not limited to, seals, other whales and dolphins, dugongs, fish, sea turtles and birds. Even land mammals may be eaten— there are records of pods killing and eating Moose and Caribou that swam across narrow channels and rivers in Canada and Alaska.

REPRODUCTION: Mating occurs between individuals of a pod—Orcas rarely breed outside their social group. Males reach maturity when they are about 19 ft (5.8 m) long, and females when they are about 16 ft (4.9 m) long. Winter appears to be the peak calving period, and gestation is believed to be 12 to 16 months.

seen straight on. Females have smaller and more curved dorsal fins than males. Behind the dorsal fin there is often a gray or purplish "saddle." An Orca's eye is located below and in front of the white facial spot. The snout tapers to a rounded point. The flukes are dark on top and whitish below, and they have pointed tips, concave trailing edges and a distinct notch in the middle. Male Orcas are much larger than females.

BLOW: In cool air, the Orca makes a low, bushy blow.

OTHER DISPLAYS: Orcas are extremely acrobatic whales for their size. They are inquisitive and often approach boats, apparently to get a better look at the humans on board. They are often seen breaching clear out of

False Killer Whale

SIMILAR SPECIES:
False Killer Whale (p. 76).

Northern Right Whale Dolphin

Lissodelphis borealis

DESCRIPTION: This unmistakable, torpedo-shaped dolphin is the only dolphin in the Northern Hemisphere that lacks a dorsal fin. It is named after the Northern Right Whale (p. 58), which also lacks a dorsal fin. This dolphin's head is narrow and its beak is pointed, with the lower jaw protruding. It has a distinctive, white "chin." The Northern Right Whale Dolphin is mainly black, dark slate gray or dark brown, and it has some white between the flippers, in the navel area and on the underside of the tail stock. The flippers are small and slender. The backward-pointing flukes are narrow, notched, dark on the dorsal side and white below.

BLOW: As with most dolphins, the blow may be audible but is not visible.

OTHER DISPLAYS: This dolphin is shy and easily startled, but in ideal circumstances it can be seen leaping clear of the water, breaching, lob-tailing and side-slapping. In one long leap, it can cover up to 23 ft (7 m). When many of these dolphins are traveling together at high speed, the water's surface resembles rapidly boiling water.

GROUP SIZE: Groups of these dolphins number between 5 and 200 individuals, but some aggregations as large as 3000 have been observed.

FEEDING: The Northern Right Whale Dolphin feeds mainly on small and mid-sized fish or squid. It takes its prey at the surface or at mid-depths—it does not feed far below the surface.

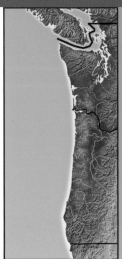

RANGE: Northern Right Whale Dolphins are found only in the North Pacific between the western coast of North America and Japan.

OTHER NAMES: Pacific Right Whale Porpoise.

STATUS: Probably common.

TOTAL LENGTH: up to 10 ft (3 m); average 8 ft (2.4 m).

TOTAL WEIGHT: up to 250 lb (110 kg); average 180 lb (82 kg).

BIRTH LENGTH: 28–39 in (71–99 cm).

BIRTH WEIGHT: unknown.

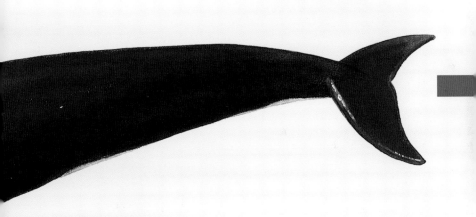

REPRODUCTION: Sexual maturity occurs when an individual is 70 to 75 percent of its adult body length, although social maturity may also be a factor in the onset of sexual activity. Little is known about the reproductive history for these dolphins, except that the peak calving time is in winter and early spring.

Striped Dolphin

SIMILAR SPECIES: Striped Dolphin (p. 64); Saddleback Dolphins (p. 66).

85

Harbor Porpoise

Phocoena phocoena

The little Harbor Porpoise is the most widespread member of its family. It favors coastal waters, such as estuaries, shallow bays and tidal channels, and it has even been seen short distances up rivers.

In the past, this porpoise was a familiar sight to boaters and sailors of coastal waters, but its population is declining. In some regions, alarming numbers of Harbor Porpoises have washed up either dead or dying. Although the reasons are not clear, many scientists suspect that high levels of toxins and pollutants impair the immune systems of these and other cetaceans, which makes them more susceptible to life-threatening diseases.

Drowning deaths are another main reason why Harbor Porpoises are declining. Because of this porpoise's feeding habits, it is frequently caught in bottom-set gill nets, a kind of net that hangs deep in the water like a curtain. Almost every kind of deep net can

RANGE: Harbor Porpoises are found in cold-temperate and subarctic waters of the Northern Hemisphere. They occur in coastal waters no deeper than 980 ft (300 m), but preferably no deeper than 660 ft (200 m).

OTHER NAMES: Common Porpoise, Puffing Porpoise.

STATUS: Declining.

TOTAL LENGTH: up to 6½ ft (2 m); average 5 ft (1.5 m).

TOTAL WEIGHT: up to 150 lb (68 kg); average 130 lb (59 kg).

BIRTH LENGTH: 26–35 in (66–89 cm).

BIRTH WEIGHT: about 11 lb (5 kg).

trap and drown a cetacean, but the most sinister are nets that have been thrown away or lost by fishermen. An untended net catches numerous cetaceans, sea turtles, fish and other sea creatures until it is so heavy that it sinks to the bottom.

The solution to this problem is not easy, but leading researchers have been working on ways to warn animals, particularly porpoises, where the nets are. Some sounds repulse Harbor Porpoises, and now a device called a "pinger" can be specially made and fitted to the nets. The pinger emits a sound that the porpoises do not like, resulting in the porpoises steering clear of the net. In the future, devices such as this one may help save the lives of thousands of porpoises and other cetaceans.

DESCRIPTION: This small porpoise is the smallest cetacean in the Pacific Northwest. Its markings are not distinct, so the best way to identify it is by general body shape, behavior and the sound it makes to breathe. It is mainly dark or slate gray over the back, fading to white underneath. In some individuals the color change is gradual, while in others the change is well defined, especially on the tail stock. Even on one individual, the color pattern may not be the same from one side to the other. The face is small, the head tapers gently and the mouth angles slightly upward. This porpoise has black "lips," and one or two black streaks lead back to its all-black flippers. The dorsal fin and flukes are black as well, and the flukes are pointed slightly backward and are notched in the middle. Upon close examination, you can see little bumps, or tubercles, on the leading edge of the dorsal fin and flippers.

BLOW: Although Harbor Porpoises are difficult to observe because they rarely show much of themselves abovewater, they make a remarkable sound when they breathe.

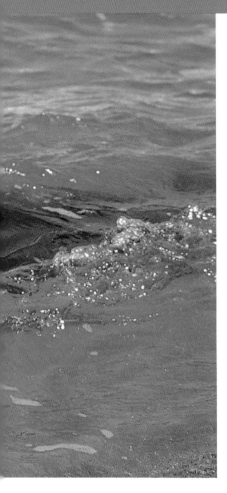

silently and motionlessly just below the surface of the water. This behavior also occurs at night, and it probably helps them remain undetected by predators. On rare occasions, Harbor Porpoises have been seen bow-riding. When they swim quickly they may "porpoise" in and out of the water.

GROUP SIZE: Harbor Porpoises usually live in small groups of two to five individuals. Some groups have up to 15 members, and good feeding waters can attract from 50 to several hundred porpoises.

FEEDING: Harbor Porpoises feed in midwater or on the bottom, and their main foods include small schooling fish, such as anchovies or herring. They rarely venture into water more than 660 ft (200 m) deep.

REPRODUCTION: Both male and female Harbor Porpoises mature sexually between the ages of three and four. Mating usually occurs in early summer, and calving is 11 months later. The newborns are dull brown in color, and for the first few hours they have "birth lines," or creases, circumscribing their bodies. This species is not long-lived; most die before they are 10 years old.

When a Harbor Porpoise breaks the surface, it makes a quick sneezing sound, which has earned it the nickname "puffing porpoise."

OTHER DISPLAYS: Like other porpoises, the Harbor Porpoise shows little of itself above-water. It rarely performs acrobatics like dolphins, and it is not as fast and active as the Dall's Porpoise (p. 90). Only its comical sneezing sound attracts the attention of whale watchers. Harbor Porpoises do not like intruders, however, and if they are uncomfortable and want to hide they will lie

Pacific White-sided Dolphin

SIMILAR SPECIES:
Pacific White-sided Dolphin (p. 70).

Dall's Porpoise

Phocoenoides dalli

The second smallest cetacean in the Pacific Northwest, the Dall's Porpoise is a welcome sight for boaters and whale watchers. It is a high-speed swimmer that frequently provides hours of delight for human spectators. Fortunately, it is very tolerant of human company, and the approach of boats rarely startles it.

Despite being a porpoise, the Dall's Porpoise does not actually "porpoise" through the water like dolphins and other small cetaceans do. Instead, it surfaces only long enough for a quick breath. In doing so, it creates the distinctive conical splash of water that is typical of this species.

Dall's Porpoises appear to undergo short migrations in the Pacific Northwest. In summer, they tend to move northward; in winter they move farther south and are commonly seen off Washington and Oregon. There may also be some inshore-offshore migration, perhaps in response to food availability. In some years, for unexplained reasons, mass assemblies of a few thousand individuals have been monitored moving through passages near Alaska.

RANGE: Dall's Porpoises are found in the North Pacific between 30° N and 62° N, both close to land and in the open sea.

OTHER NAMES: Spray Porpoise, True's Porpoise, White-flanked Porpoise.

STATUS: Common but declining.

TOTAL LENGTH: up to 8 ft (2.4 m); average 6 ft (1.8 m).

TOTAL WEIGHT: up to 490 lb (220 kg); average 300 lb (140 kg).

BIRTH LENGTH: 2½–3 ft (76–91 cm).

BIRTH WEIGHT: unknown.

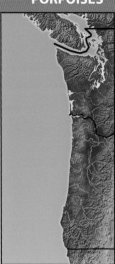

Like all dolphins and porpoises, Dall's Porpoises have the ability to rest just half of their brain at a time, which allows them to keep a constant state of awareness to remain vigilant for dangers. The major natural predators to Dall's Porpoises are Orcas (p. 80) and sharks.

Worldwide efforts to protect whales have had many admirable results. Unfortunately, the Dall's Porpoise is still being hunted on a massive scale. Several countries take a total of at least 14,000—and sometimes as many as 45,000—Dall's Porpoises every year. Moreover, several thousand more porpoises are accidentally killed in fishing nets. These numbers are extremely high, and it is likely that the total population cannot sustain such losses.

DESCRIPTION: Often mistaken for a baby Orca by boaters, the Dall's Porpoise is distinctly colored black and white. Its head is black and tapers to a narrow mouth. Its "lips" are usually black, but on some individuals they are white. The black body is extremely robust for its length. There is a large white patch on the belly and sides: on some individuals it stretches from in front of the flippers

Top view of tail

to the tail stock; on others it begins about one-third of the way down the body. The black, triangular dorsal fin has a hooked tip, and it is usually light gray or white on the trailing half. The small flippers lie close to the head, and they are dark black on both sides. When viewed from above, the tail is shaped like a wide gingko leaf, and it has a white or gray trailing edge.

BLOW: When breathing, this porpoise does not make a visible blow. As it swims and darts and zigzags about. It seems to love bow-riding, and it will zoom toward a fast-moving boat like a black-and-white torpedo. If a Dall's Porpoise comes to the bow of your boat, don't slow down for a better look, because it quickly loses interest in boats going slower than about 12 mph (19 km/h).

GROUP SIZE: Dall's Porpoises are commonly found in groups of 10 to 20 individuals, although meetings of hundreds or even thousands may occur in some waters.

FEEDING: The Dall's Porpoise feeds both at the surface and in deep water. Its primary foods include squid, lanternfish, hake, mackerel, capelin and other schooling fish. Its maximum feeding depth has been estimated at about 1600 ft (490 m). This porpoise has a high metabolic rate and requires large amounts of food at frequent intervals.

REPRODUCTION: Males reach sexual maturity when they are about 6 ft (1.8 m) long; females when they are 5$^1/_2$ ft (1.7 m) long. Observations indicate two peaks in calving, one in February-March and another in July-August. Peak mating must have a similar split, because the gestation period is about 11$^1/_2$ months.

breaks the surface, a V-shaped cone of water comes off its head. Many boaters look for this "rooster-tail" to locate the porpoises, because it can be seen from a great distance away, even though the porpoise itself is not visible.

OTHER DISPLAYS: The Dall's Porpoise is not acrobatic and does not leap out of the water. Nevertheless, it is exceptionally fast—it is often clocked at speeds of up to 35 mph (56 km/h)—and it even seems hyperactive as it

Pacific White-sided Dolphin

SIMILAR SPECIES: Pacific White-sided Dolphin (p. 70); newborn Orca (p. 80).

Baird's Beaked Whale

Berardius bairdii

DESCRIPTION: The largest of the beaked whales, the Baird's Beaked Whale has an elongated, spindle-shaped body. It is mainly slate gray or dark brownish in color, and it typically has many light-colored scars over its sides and back. There are variable light-colored blotches on its undersides. It has a very small, stubby dorsal fin set far back on the dorsal ridge. The small, rounded flippers are set close to the head. The flukes are also small, and they have almost straight trailing edges. The beak is distinct, with the lower jaw protruding. The four teeth of the lower jaw are visible even when the mouth is closed. The forehead has a prominent bulge, and the blowhole is indented. Female Baird's Beaked Whales are generally larger than males.

BLOW: This large whale makes a small, bushy blow that is sometimes visible.

OTHER DISPLAYS: A pod of Baird's Beaked Whales travels in synchrony, rising and blowing at the same time. When they surface to breathe, the blow is quick, and the blowhole disappears before the dorsal fin or hump emerges. On rare occasions, these whales are seen breaching, spy-hopping and lob-tailing.

GROUP SIZE: Baird's Beaked Whales are often seen in groups of 3 to 50 individuals. Large groups may temporarily break up into smaller pods and later rejoin.

RANGE: Baird's Beaked Whales are found in the North Pacific Ocean and the Japan, Okhotsk and Bering seas.

OTHER NAMES: Giant Bottlenosed Whale, North Pacific Great Bottle-nosed Whale, Giant Four-toothed Whale, Northern Four-toothed Whale.

STATUS: Probably stable; insufficient data worldwide.

TOTAL LENGTH: up to 42 ft (13 m); average 38 ft (12 m).

TOTAL WEIGHT: up to 15 tons (13,600 kg); average 12 tons (10,900 kg).

BIRTH LENGTH: 14–15 ft (4.3–4.6 m).

BIRTH WEIGHT: unknown.

FEEDING: Baird's Beaked Whales feed on bottom-dwelling creatures, such as skates, crustaceans and squid. They avoid deep oceans and favor areas above the continental shelf or around seamounts, where the bottom is accessible and food is more abundant.

REPRODUCTION: Both males and females are sexually mature at 80 to 85 percent of their adult length. Gestation is estimated to be about 17 months, and the peak calving period is in March and April. Very little else is known about the mating habits of these whales.

SIMILAR SPECIES: The Baird's Beaked Whale is twice the size of other beaked whales in the region, so only a juvenile Baird's could be confused with another beaked whale.

Cuvier's Beaked Whale

Ziphius cavirostris

DESCRIPTION: This whale is medium-sized and its color is highly variable, including cream, beige, brown and purplish or reddish black. The color pattern is swirled and blotchy, and most individuals have spots and scars along their sides and undersides. The head is triangular, with an indistinct beak and two small teeth on the lower, protruding jaw. The flippers are small and set close to the head, while the dorsal fin is small and set close to the tail. The flukes are pointed, only slightly notched in the middle and broad—almost a quarter of the length of the body. Female Cuvier's Beaked Whales are generally larger than males.

BLOW: The blow is usually invisible, but it may be seen after a long dive. It is low and bushy, and it generally points forward and to the left.

OTHER DISPLAYS: This beaked whale breaches infrequently, rising vertically and completely out of the water and falling ungracefully back in. It usually avoid boats and whale watchers, but there are a few notable cases where inquisitive individuals have approached boats.

GROUP SIZE: When solitary Cuvier's Beaked Whales are seen, they are usually old males. Normally, these whales form groups of 2 to 10 members, but pods as large as 25 have been recorded.

FEEDING: Cuvier's Beaked Whales make deep dives of 20 to 40 minutes to feed on deep-sea fish and squid. They are rarely seen close to land.

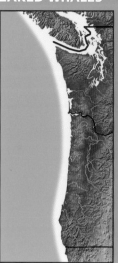

RANGE: The Cuvier's Beaked Whale is found throughout the world, in all seas except the cold polar waters. It is the most widespread member of its family, and probably the most common.

OTHER NAMES: Goose-beaked Whale, Cuvier's Whale.

STATUS: Insufficiently known.

TOTAL LENGTH: up to 23 ft (7 m); average 20 ft (6.1 m).

TOTAL WEIGHT: up to 3½ tons (3200 kg); average 2½ tons (2300 kg).

BIRTH LENGTH: 6½–9½ ft (2–2.9 m).

BIRTH WEIGHT: about 550 lb (250 kg).

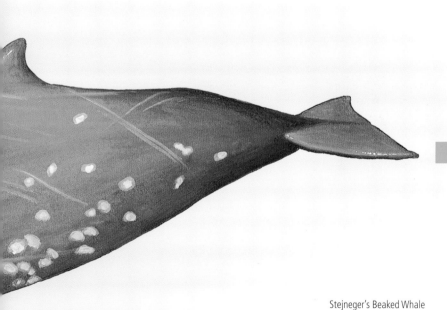

Stejneger's Beaked Whale

REPRODUCTION: Sexually maturity for both males and females is reached at about 75 percent of the adult length. The peak periods for mating and calving are unknown, because these whales are poorly understood in the wild.

SIMILAR SPECIES:
Stejneger's Beaked Whale (p. 100).

Hubbs's Beaked Whale

Mesoplodon carlhubbsi

DESCRIPTION: To quickly identify this whale at sea, a male must be seen, because males have distinct, white facial markings. The females are nondescript shades of gray, but the males have bulging white foreheads and stocky white beaks. Two massive teeth are visible on either side of the jaw, even if the mouth is closed. Many long scars and white spots are typically seen over the dark gray body. The flippers are small and set close to the head, and the dorsal fin is small, curved and sits about two-thirds of the way back along the dorsal ridge. The flukes are lighter below than above, and they are slightly pointed but rarely notched. Information about this species has been gathered from a few stranded individuals.

BLOW: This whale probably raises its head clear of the water to breathe, but no accurate data is known.

OTHER DISPLAYS: Although this whale probably partakes in abovewater displays, humans have not seen it enough to document its behavior.

GROUP SIZE: Only one positive sighting of this whale has been recorded, so the details of its group and social behavior remain a mystery.

FEEDING: Like many other members of this family, the Hubbs's Beaked Whale probably feeds on squid and deepwater fish.

Male

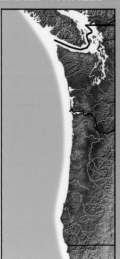

RANGE: The Hubbs's Beaked Whale lives in the deep, open water of the North Pacific around Japan and the western coast of Canada and the United States.

OTHER NAMES: Arch-beaked Whale.

STATUS: Insufficiently known.

TOTAL LENGTH: up to 18 ft (5.5 m); average 17 ft (5.2 m).

TOTAL WEIGHT: up to 1.7 tons (1500 kg); average 1.3 tons (1200 kg).

BIRTH LENGTH: 7½–8½ ft (2.3–2.6 m).

BIRTH WEIGHT: unknown.

Stejneger's Beaked Whale

REPRODUCTION: Because this whale is so infrequently encountered in the wild, virtually nothing is known about its reproduction or mating behavior. It is believed that calving occurs in mid-summer.

SIMILAR SPECIES:
Stejneger's Beaked Whale (p. 100).

Stejneger's Beaked Whale

Mesoplodon stejnegeri

DESCRIPTION: This dark gray or nearly black beaked whale has a pointed head without a distinct bulge on the forehead. Females and young, which are difficult to distinguish from each other, are uniformly dark gray, with paler undersides. Some juveniles may have light streaks in the neck region. Males have two prominent lower teeth and a distinct, pale gray beak and lower jaw. The erupted teeth on the male's lower jaw produce a strongly curved mouth line. These teeth may curve over the upper jaw on older individuals. The flippers are small and narrow, and the dorsal fin is small and triangular. The flukes are wide and triangular, with a nearly straight trailing edge.

BLOW: The Stejneger's Beaked Whale makes an inconspicuous, small blow. After a deep dive, its blow may be visible.

OTHER DISPLAYS: This whale is not very approachable, and it tends to vacate an area when boats are around. Its dive sequence involves a simple roll at the surface, which exposes little of the body. Other displays have not been documented but probably occur infrequently.

GROUP SIZE: This whale commonly forms groups of two to five members. Some groups may have as many as 15 members.

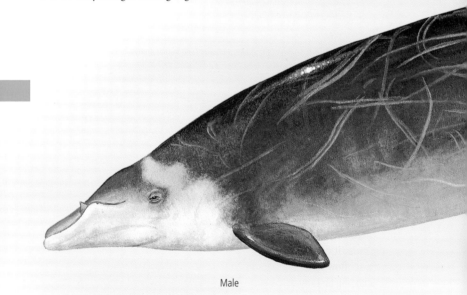

Male

100

RANGE: Stejneger's Beaked Whales can be found in cold and subarctic waters of the North Pacific and the Sea of Japan.

OTHER NAMES: Saber-toothed Whale, Bering Sea Beaked Whale, North Pacific Beaked Whale.

STATUS: Insufficiently known; probably very rare.

TOTAL LENGTH: up to 17 ft (5.2 m); average 16 ft (4.9 m).

TOTAL WEIGHT: up to 1.3 tons (1200 kg); average 1.2 tons (1100 kg).

BIRTH LENGTH: about 5 ft (1.5 m).

BIRTH WEIGHT: unknown.

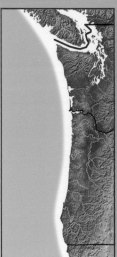

FEEDING: The Stejneger's Beaked Whale probably feeds on deepwater fish and squid. When it dives for food, it first performs a series of five or six shallow dives and then one long, deep dive lasting up to 15 minutes.

REPRODUCTION: Nothing is known about the mating behavior and reproductive history of this whale.

Cuvier's Beaked Whale

SIMILAR SPECIES: Cuvier's Beaked Whale (p. 96); Hubbs's Beaked Whale (p. 98).

Pygmy Sperm Whale

Kogia breviceps

DESCRIPTION: Like its close relative, the Dwarf Sperm Whale (p. 104), this small whale is almost shark-like in appearance. It has a protruding snout and an underslung lower jaw, and many individuals have a streak behind the eye that resembles a gill slit. The blowhole is on top of the head and displaced slightly to the left. The dorsal fin is tiny, slender and curved, and the flippers are broad and almond shaped. The tail flukes are convex and notched, with distinctly pointed tips. The overall body color is slate blue, dark gray or even brownish, and the undersides are nearly white.

BLOW: These whales make small, inconspicuous blows that are visible only on clear, calm days and at close range.

OTHER DISPLAYS: When they surface to breathe, Pygmy Sperm Whales are very inconspicuous and usually drop back under immediately. These whales may occasionally breach, and they typically fall back into the water with little grace. They sometimes release a cloud of dark intestinal fluid that probably serves either to distract intruders or to confuse prey.

GROUP SIZE: Pygmy Sperm Whales live in small groups of three to six members. Rarely, they are observed singly or in groups as large as 10 individuals.

FEEDING: The Pygmy Sperm Whale feeds mainly in deep water, catching such creatures as squid, fish and some crustaceans.

RANGE: Pygmy Sperm Whales are widespread in deep, tropical, subtropical and temperate waters. Their distribution is patchy and insufficiently known.

OTHER NAMES: Lesser Sperm Whale, Lesser Cachalot, Short-headed Whale.

STATUS: Insufficiently known.

TOTAL LENGTH: up to 12 ft (3.7 m); average 10 ft (3 m).

TOTAL WEIGHT: up to 900 lb (410 kg); average 780 lb (350 kg).

BIRTH LENGTH: about 4 ft (1.2 m).

BIRTH WEIGHT: about 120 lb (54 kg).

REPRODUCTION: Length at sexually maturity is believed to be about 9 ft (2.7 m) for Pygmy Sperm Whales. Calving and mating may occur year-round, but little accurate data exist for this species.

Dwarf Sperm Whale

SIMILAR SPECIES:
Dwarf Sperm Whale (p. 104).

103

Dwarf Sperm Whale

Kogia simus

DESCRIPTION: This unusual whale resembles a slightly fat shark. Its snout is short and squarish, and its mouth is tiny and underslung. There is a white streak behind the eye that resembles the gill slit on a shark. Overall, the body is dark or bluish gray, with lighter undersides. The flippers are short and broad, and the dorsal fin, which is larger than that of the Pygmy Sperm Whale (p. 102), is pointed and has a concave trailing edge. The flukes are broad, pointed and notched in the middle. The blowhole is set above the eye and slightly displaced to the left.

BLOW: The Dwarf Sperm Whale does not make a distinct blow.

OTHER DISPLAYS: When this whale rises to breathe, it does not roll forward into a dive like other whales; instead, it takes a quick breath and then simply drops out of sight. It may be seen resting at the surface, and it occasionally breaches—rising vertically out of the water and splashing back haphazardly. When startled, it may release a cloud of dark intestinal fluid that presumably distracts an intruder while it dives. These clouds may also be released to confuse prey.

GROUP SIZE: Dwarf Sperm Whales travel alone or in pairs. On occasion, they have been seen in groups of up to 10 individuals.

FEEDING: This whale has a small mouth and presumably eats small creatures. Its primary foods are thought to be cuttlefish, squid and fish.

RANGE: Dwarf Sperm Whales can be seen in a number of locations throughout deep temperate, subtropical and tropical waters in both the Northern and Southern hemispheres. Their distribution is probably patchy rather than continuous.

STATUS: Insufficiently known; probably stable.

TOTAL LENGTH: up to 9 ft (2.7 m); average 8 ft (2.4 m).

TOTAL WEIGHT: up to 610 lb (280 kg); average 450 lb (200 kg).

BIRTH LENGTH: about 39 in (1 m).

BIRTH WEIGHT: 90–110 lb (41–50 kg).

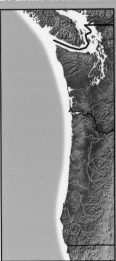

Pygmy Sperm Whale

REPRODUCTION: The gestation period for this whale is about nine months, and calving is at its peak during the summer months. Both sexes reach maturity when they are 75 to 80 percent of their adult length.

SIMILAR SPECIES: Pygmy Sperm Whale (p. 102); Risso's Dolphin (p. 74).

Sperm Whale

Physeter macrocephalus

The famous Sperm Whale is a definite record-breaker in the world of mammals. It is easily the deepest-diving mammal on Earth, and it can hold its breath for more than two hours. Sperm Whales may not have a maximum diving depth, because greater and greater dives keep being recorded. The restricting factor appears to be the time without oxygen, rather than the enormous pressure on the body. At 10,500 ft (3200 m), which is believed to be the deepest recorded dive, the pressure on the body is a staggering 317 atmospheres, yet Sperm Whales are still able to function.

The Sperm Whale's biggest adaptation to surviving these pressures is that before it dives, it removes the air from its lungs to help minimize the difference in pressure between its body cavities and the surrounding water. Because the whale's body, like ours, is mainly water, it resists compression.

The mammoth head of the Sperm Whale is filled with very fine quality oil, called spermaceti, and it may function to

Male

DIVE SEQUENCE

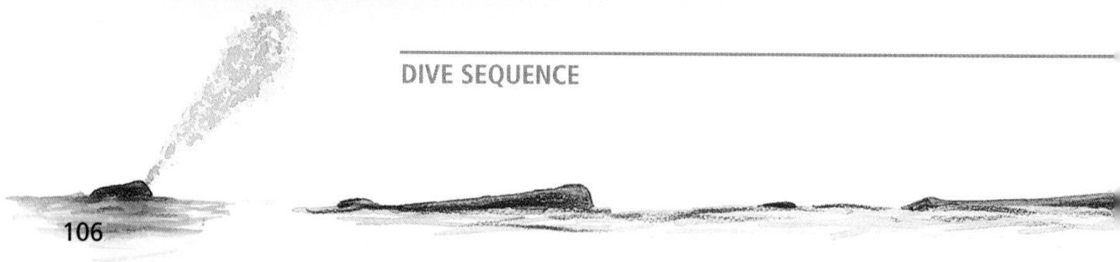

RANGE: The Sperm Whale can be found in deep waters worldwide. Although it is widespread, its distribution is probably patchy.

OTHER NAMES: Cachalot, Anvil-headed Whale.

STATUS: Endangered (FWS); locally stable in some waters.

TOTAL LENGTH: up to 69 ft (21 m); average 48 ft (15 m).

TOTAL WEIGHT: up to 58 tons (53,000 kg); average 35 tons (32,000 kg).

BIRTH LENGTH: about 13 ft (4 m).

BIRTH WEIGHT: about 1 ton (910 kg).

regulate the whale's buoyancy as it dives and surfaces. The other proposed theory is that the spermaceti serves to magnify or focus the whale's sound emission during echolocation. Perhaps the spermaceti performs both of these functions for the whale.

Females have dramatically smaller heads than males, but the reason for this difference is not clearly understood. Females also dive deeply and rely on echolocation, so perhaps the larger head of the male serves another purpose.

DESCRIPTION: The Sperm Whale is easy to recognize because of its extremely large head and distinctive features. The head is as much as one-third of the total body length. It is narrow when seen from above and rectangular when seen from the side. A male has a much larger and more rectangular head than a female. The eyes are relatively small and inconspicuous. The mouth and tip of the snout may be white or light gray, and scarring may be obvious. The blowhole is slightly raised at the end of the snout, and it is displaced to the left. The overall body color is brown, gray or nearly black, but the undersides are often lighter. The stubby flippers and broad, triangular tail flukes are dark on both sides, but scarring may lighten the edges. The trailing edge of the flukes is sometimes scalloped, and such variations in the tail are used by researchers to identify individuals. Instead of a true dorsal fin, the Sperm Whale has a distinct hump or knuckle where the fin should be. Several smaller knuckles continue down the dorsal ridge to the tail. The skin appears "pruney" from behind the eye to the tail stock. Male Sperm Whales are much larger than females.

BLOW: Because the blowhole of the Sperm Whale is at the tip of the snout and displaced to the left, the blow sprays forward and to the left. No other whale makes a blow like this, so even from afar a Sperm Whale can be identified.

OTHER DISPLAYS: Sperm Whales may breach and lob-tail, especially juveniles.

dives is from two Sperm Whales that were believed to reach 10,500 ft (3200 m), where they consumed bottom-dwelling sharks. The main foods eaten by Sperm Whales are squid and Giant Squid, octopus, large fish and sharks. Sperm Whales locate their food in the darkness of deep water by using their extremely sophisticated echolocation.

REPRODUCTION: Although males are sexually mature when they are about 10 years old, they are unlikely to mate for several more years. Females are sexually mature when they are 8 to 12 years old. Mating usually occurs in late winter or early spring, and single calves are born in summer or fall, following a gestation of 14 to 15 months. The young may nurse for several years, even after they start eating solid food.

When they return from a deep dive, they breathe at the surface 30 or 40 times before diving again. The first breath is very loud and explosive, while the subsequent breaths are quieter. Between dives, the whales usually stay at the surface for about 15 minutes, but sometimes they will remain near the surface for as long as an hour.

GROUP SIZE: Sperm Whales usually live in groups of 2 to 25 animals. Nursery colonies of females and young number 12 to 30 individuals, and bachelor colonies of many young males are also common. At times, assemblages of hundreds or even thousands of Sperm Whales have been reported.

FEEDING: The ability of the Sperm Whale to feed at great depths is unsurpassed by any other mammal. One of the deepest recorded

Humpback Whale

SIMILAR SPECIES: Humpback Whale (p. 54), during the dive sequence.

Seals and Otters

During a trip on the waters off Washington and Oregon, you may see several mammals other than whales, including seals, sea-lions and otters. Although these other marine mammals are highly adapted to life in the ocean, unlike whales, they are able to come ashore at any time. All seals, sea-lions and otters are members of the order Carnivora, as are dogs, cats, bears and weasels, among others.

Outwardly, all the seals look similar, and they were once classified in their own order, Pinnipedia, meaning "fin feet." Further study revealed that seal-like mammals are actually a good example of convergent evolution, where creatures of different origins look or function similarly because of comparable adaptations to a common problem. There are two distinct lineages of seals: the eared seals (and their later offshoot, the Walrus) likely share a common ancestor with bears; the hair seals are descendants of an ancestral member of the weasel family. Despite having different lineages, all seals and sea-lions are still frequently referred to as pinnipeds.

EARED SEAL FAMILY (OTARIIDAE)

This family, which is found almost worldwide, includes the fur seals and the sea-lions. At a glance, it should be easy to tell this family of seals from the hair seals: all the eared seals have small but noticeable external ears, whereas the hair seals do not. As well, the eared seals can rotate their hindlimbs forward into a more leg-like position, which enables them to walk or even lope when on shore. Another good way to identify members of this family is that none of them has distinct markings on its fur. Although their coats may vary in color from light to dark brown or gray, there are no rings, spots or patterns. Eared seals have large, thick, hairless flippers with well-developed claws on the middle three digits of the hind flippers.

Northern Fur Seal

HAIR SEAL FAMILY (PHOCIDAE)

The hair seals are also referred to as either the earless seals or the "true" seals. As the former name suggests, they have no visible external ears. The best way to distinguish these seals from the eared seals, however, is by body shape. The hind flippers of hair seals are permanently pointed backward—these seals are unable to rotate their hindlimbs forward to help support their body weight when they are on land. As a result, on land hair seals move with clumsy undulations of their bodies. Once in the water, hair seals are graceful, lithe swimmers capable of high speeds and rapid turns. Their forelimbs are small compared to those of eared seals, but the flippers are strong enough that the seal can hold itself upright and tread water at the surface. Members of this family all have hair on their flippers and claws on all five digits of each flipper.

Northern Elephant Seal

OTTER SUBFAMILY (LUTRINAE)

Otters are a subgroup of the weasel family (Mustelidae), which also includes terrestrial carnivores, such as minks, weasels, badgers and martens. There are two otters in North America: the Sea Otter and the Northern River Otter. The Sea Otter, which can be seen along certain parts of the Washington and Oregon coasts, spends almost its entire life in the water. It mates in the water, and females give birth and nurse their young in the water. Sea Otters typically only come ashore to wait out bad storms. The Northern River Otter is similar to the Sea Otter, except that it is smaller, slimmer and has a longer tail. Although the Northern River Otter typically inhabits fresh water and is not strictly a marine mammal, it is seen on the coast more often than the Sea Otter.

Sea Otter

Northern Fur Seal

Callorhinus ursinus

DESCRIPTION: The Northern Fur Seal has a small head, a short, pointed nose with long whiskers, small ears, large eyes and a very short tail. The front flippers are extremely large compared to the size of the body. When this seal is wet it looks sleek and black; when dry, males are mostly dark grayish black, while females show a brownish throat and often some silvery gray underparts. Adult males have a thickened neck and are more than twice the weight of females. Newborn pups are black.

Male

RANGE: This wide-ranging species may undergo annual migrations of up to 6200 mi (10,000 km). It is found from California up the West Coast and across the North Pacific to Japan.

STATUS: Declining.

TOTAL LENGTH: male 6–7½ ft (1.8–2.3 m); female 3½–5 ft (1.1–1.5 m).

TAIL LENGTH: 2 in (5.1 cm).

TOTAL WEIGHT: male 330–620 lb (150–280 kg); female 85–120 lb (39–54 kg).

HABITAT: This seal is pelagic for 7 to 10 months of the year. It rests at sea by floating on its back, with its hind flippers bent up and laid onto its belly and held down by the fore flippers. It comes ashore only to breed, mainly on rocky beaches of isolated northern islands.

FEEDING: Northern Fur Seals feed mainly on squid, herring, capelin and pollack up to 10 in (25 cm) long. Almost all feeding activity occurs at night.

REPRODUCTION: Males come ashore in late May and June and battle to establish their territories. Females come ashore in mid-June or July, and within two days they give birth to a pup that was conceived the previous summer. Mating occurs 8 to 10 days after the pup is born. The pup nurses for only four or five months.

Harbor Seal

SIMILAR SPECIES: Harbor Seal (p. 122); Northern Sea-Lion (p. 114).

113

Northern Sea-Lion

Eumetopias jubatus

The large Northern Sea-Lion is a familiar sight to many people who frequent coastal waters. It may be seen basking on shore or resting in the water in a vertical position, with its head above the surface. This pinniped is quite gregarious—it is usually seen in groups numbering a few hundred to thousands of individuals—and its social system is more advanced than that of the Harbor Seal (p. 122), which is another common pinniped of the Pacific Northwest. For example, when a group of sea-lions is feeding, they all dive at the same time and all surface together, as well, which means that no individual dives first and scares the fish away, ruining the feeding opportunities for the others.

There is great sexual dimorphism in sea-lions, and males are three to four times as heavy as females—adult male Northern Sea-Lions are the largest of the eared seals. A large difference in weight is characteristic of seals with territorial males that hold a harem. Females form loose aggregations with their pups within a male's territory, and they are far faster and more agile than the males.

During the breeding and pupping season, hundreds of sea-lions congregate at rookery sites used by generations of sea-lions.

Male

RANGE: Northern Sea-Lions are found near the shore from southern California up to Alaska, through the Aleutian Islands to Siberia and south to Japan.

OTHER NAMES: Steller Sea-Lion.

STATUS: Declining; endangered (FWS) in some parts of its range.

TOTAL LENGTH: male 8½–11 ft (2.6–3.4 m); female 6–7 ft (1.8–2.1 m).

TOTAL WEIGHT: male up to 2200 lb (1000 kg); female 600–800 lb (270–360 kg).

Mature bulls make a roaring sound at this time, and, combined with the grumbles and growls of other colony members, the resulting cacophony can be heard for more than ¹/₂ mi (800 m). Adult males evicted from the breeding colony often bear huge cuts and tears on the neck and chest—reminders of the vicious battles waged over a territory. Outside the pupping season, the "bachelors," the young of that year, some barren cows and the odd mature bull form loose colonies.

The Northern Sea-Lion is well noted for its exceptional curiosity and playfulness. It sometimes leaps clear from the water—it has even been seen jumping across surfaced whales—and it occasionally throws rocks back and forth. The smaller California Sea-Lion (p. 118), which shares this playfulness, is commonly seen performing tricks in marine park shows.

For many years, sea-lions were killed because it was believed that they fed on commercially valuable fish. Recent research indicates that they feed opportunistically on any available fish; common prey include octopus, squid and "scrap" fish, such as herring and greenling. Although the intentional killing of sea-lions has decreased, their populations have continued to decline by as much as 80 percent from historic numbers. The causes of this decline are unknown.

A unique characteristic of sea-lions is that they frequently swallow rocks as large as 5 in (13 cm) across. Although no one knows for sure, the most likely explanation is that the stones help pulverize food inside a sea-lion's stomach. A sea-lion's teeth are ill-suited to chewing, and it regularly swallows large chunks of meat and whole fish.

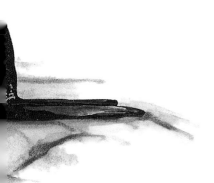

DESCRIPTION: Adults are light buff to reddish brown when dry, and brown to nearly black when wet. Males, which are much larger than females, develop a huge neck that supports a mane of long, coarse hair. Females are sleek. The hind flippers can be drawn forward under the body, and, like all eared seals, sea-lions can jump and clamber up steep rocky slopes at an amazing rate. The fore flippers are strong and are used for propulsion underwater.

HABITAT: Northern Sea-Lions live mainly in coastal waters near rocky shores. They are known to swim up large rivers in search of food. Sea-lions are seldom found more than 150 ft (46 m) from water, and they prefer to stay in the ocean during inclement weather. When it is sunny, they usually haul out and bask on rocky shores.

FEEDING: These sea-lions feed primarily on fish, such as blackfish, greenling, rockfish and herring. Others foods include squid, octopus, shrimp, clams, salmon and bottom fish. In parts of Oregon and Washington, these sea-lions are known to swim short distances up rivers in search of an easy meal, such as lamprey. Male sea-lions do not eat for one to two months while they are defending a territory.

REPRODUCTION: Males come ashore in early May and battle to establish their territories on rocky, boulder-strewn beaches or rock ledges. Females come ashore in mid-May or June, and within three days they give birth to a pup conceived during the previous summer. Mating occurs within two weeks after the pup is born. The pup typically nurses for about one year, but some have been known to nurse for as long as three years. Females may live to be 30 years old and are sexually mature at three to seven years. Males probably do not breed before age 10.

California Sea-Lion

SIMILAR SPECIES: California Sea-Lion (p. 118); Northern Elephant Seal (p. 126); Northern Fur Seal (p. 112).

California Sea-Lion

Zalophus californianus

The famous California Sea-Lion has received both our admiration and our persecution. Each year, thousands of children and adults watch in awe as these sea-lions flip in the air and perform stunts with hoops and big red beach balls. Sea-lions are major attractions at marine aquariums around the world, and, at best, these performances leave lasting impressions of the talent and special intrigue of our fellow mammals. Unfortunately, these good feelings are not always shared by the animal, and many sea-lions in captivity die from health problems or accidents.

In the wild, the California Sea-Lion is a playful and intelligent creature. Many visitors to coastal areas are rewarded with

Male

RANGE: The California Sea-Lion inhabits coastal waters of the North Pacific from Mexico to Vancouver Island. There are three small, isolated populations in the Sea of Japan.

STATUS: Vulnerable and declining.

TOTAL LENGTH: male 6½–8 ft (2–2.4 m); female 4½–6½ ft (1.4–2 m).

TOTAL WEIGHT: male 440–860 lb (200–390 kg); female 100–250 lb (45–110 kg).

SEALS & OTTERS

sightings of this graceful sea-lion, and lucky individuals have even had personal encounters. Kayakers and even swimmers have been approached by juveniles and females that want play. The behavior of juveniles and females is rarely aggressive, and most circumstances of play involve friendly splashes and eager somersaults underwater.

Along the coasts of Washington and Oregon, wintering California Sea-Lions may be encountered from August to April. The breeding season lasts from May to July, but their breeding grounds are much farther south. Many seal-lions leave their southern breeding territories and move northward to feed in the food-rich waters. Some females may stay near their breeding grounds all year, while younger males are more likely to be found at the northern limits of their range during winter. These sea-lions do not stay at sea for extended periods during their winter feeding; they are frequently observed at well-used haul out sites.

Despite being much adored by children and tourists, the California Sea-Lion often suffers harsh judgments in the wild. Because sea-lions potentially feed on many fish valuable to fisheries, there is widespread interaction between them and fishermen. In the 19th and early 20th centuries, California Sea-Lions were killed in great numbers for oil (from their blubber) and hides. Later in the 20th century, they were also killed for the pet food industry.

The California Sea-Lion, like all other marine mammals, is now protected by law, but each year thousand of sea-lions still die. Most of these deaths are attributable to fishing nets, discarded net material and fibrous garbage, all of which entrap and drown sea-lions. Because of intentional and accidental deaths, the California Sea-Lion population is much reduced from historical numbers, and the species may never fully recover.

DESCRIPTION: The California Sea-Lion has an elongated, slender body, a blunt snout and a short but distinct tail. Adult males are brown, and they develop a noticeably raised forehead that helps distinguish them from male Northern Sea-Lions (p. 114). Females are generally tan, with a slightly darker chest and abdomen. The coarse guard hairs of the coat cover only a small amount of underfur. The front flippers are long and bear distinct claws. California Sea-Lions are a noisy bunch—the males produce a honking bark, the cows wail and growl and the pups bleat.

HABITAT: California Sea-Lions are normally seen in coastal waters around islands with rocky or sandy beaches. Preferred haul-out sites include sandy or boulder-strewn beaches below rocky cliffs. In some places they occupy sea caverns. They tend to avoid the rocky islets preferred by Northern Sea-Lions.

FEEDING: These sea-lions eat a wide variety of foods, including at least 50 species of fish and many types of squid, octopus and other mollusks. In some regions, such as Seattle, sea-lions may feed on the endangered Steelhead Trout and other fish. Although some agencies support killing these sea-lions, there are widespread efforts for non-lethal management, such as relocating the sea-lions to distant waters.

REPRODUCTION: Males establish their territories on rocky or sandy beaches in May, June or July in warmer regions south of Oregon. Females arrive on the breeding grounds in May or June. If a female conceived the previous year, she will give birth to a pup, and within one month she mates again. Females with pups form colonies, and when a mother leaves her pup to feed, it is no easy task finding her pup amidst dozens of look-alike youngsters when she returns. First she lets out a loud, distinctive wail, and her pup will answer with a lamb-like bleat. She follows this bleat until she finds the pup, and she confirms it is hers by smell. Most pups are weaned by eight months, but a few may nurse for a year or more. They start eating fish before they are weaned.

Northern Sea-Lion

SIMILAR SPECIES: Northern Sea-Lion (p. 114); Northern Fur Seal (p. 112).

Harbor Seal

Phoca vitulina

The inquisitive Harbor Seal is a well-known resident of the Pacific Northwest. This seal bespeckles the rocky coastline at almost any time of the day throughout the year. It basks on shore either alone or in groups numbering up to the thousands.

Although many Harbor Seals may bask on rocks together, they pay very little attention to their neighbors and seldom interact. Only during the pupping season is there interaction, and it is primarily between the females. Females with newborn pups may congregate in a "nursery" in shallow water where the pups can sleep. The pups and the females sleep underwater, rising occasionally for a breath. These nursery groups are not interactive, however, but simply a precautionary measure against predators—while most of the females and pups are sleeping, some are likely to be awake and watchful for danger. The same is true for hauled-out seals. Where several seals are together, the chances are good that there is always at least one individual awake and wary of approaching danger.

Harbor Seals tend to be cautious of humans, and if you approach them on land they are likely to dive immediately into the

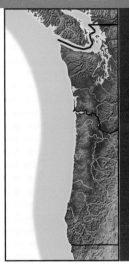

RANGE: Harbor Seals are found along the northern coasts of North America, Europe and Asia. They inhabit the entire coast of Washington and Oregon.

STATUS: Common.

TOTAL LENGTH: 4–6 ft (1.2–1.8 m).

TAIL LENGTH: 3½–4½ ft (9–11 cm).

TOTAL WEIGHT: 110–310 lb (50–140 kg).

SEALS & OTTERS

water. Many kayakers and boaters, however, have enjoyed watching inquisitive individuals that approach their boats for a better look. This kind of encounter is controlled by the seal: if it wants to see you, it will come closer; if it is afraid of you, it will leave. Do not approach a seal that has tried to flee you, because it can cause unnecessary stress on the animal.

When the tide is out at night, Harbor Seals sleep high and dry at favorite haul-out sites. They frequently rest with their heads and rear flippers lifted above the rocks. During the day, they can sleep underwater in shallow coastal water by resting vertically just above the bottom. Young pups commonly rest in this manner. Harbor Seals can go without breathing for nearly 30 minutes, and although they sometimes wake up to breathe, they frequently rise to the surface, take a breath and then sink back to the bottom without waking. Harbor Seals are unable to sleep at the surface like sea-lions (pp. 114 & 118) and Sea Otters (p. 130) can.

DESCRIPTION: The Harbor Seal is typically dark gray or brownish gray with light, blotchy spots or rings, but individuals may have the reverse color pattern—light gray or nearly white with dark spots. The undersides are generally lighter than the back. The outer coat is composed of stiff guard hairs about 3/8 in (1 cm) long, which is the characteristic that gives seals of this family the name "hair seals." The guard hairs cover an undercoat of sparse, curly hair, about 1/4 in (6 mm) long, that helps provide insulation for the seal. Pups bear a spotted, silvery or gray-brown coat at birth. The head is large, round and very dog-like, except that there are no visible ears. Each of the short front flippers has long, narrow claws. Male Harbor Seals are generally larger than females.

HABITAT: This near-shore seal is frequently found in bays and estuaries. Favored haul-out sites, which are traditionally used by many generations of Harbor Seals, commonly include intertidal sandbars, rocks

consume more shrimp and mollusks than do adults. Adult Harbor Seals have been seen taking fish from nets, and some have even entered fish traps to feed and then easily departed.

REPRODUCTION: The breeding season for Harbor Seals varies geographically. The farther north a population is located, the later its breeding and pupping occurs. Gestation lasts 10 months, and a single pup is born between April and August. The pups are weaned when they are four to six weeks old, after they have tripled their birth weight on their mother's milk, which is more than 50 percent fat. Within a few days of weaning her pup, a female mates again. Harbor Seals become sexually mature anywhere from three to seven years of age. Captive seals have lived more than 35 years, although the typical lifespan for males is 20 years and for females is 30 years.

and rocky shores. The Harbor Seal sometimes follows fish several hundred miles up major rivers, and there are even populations in some inland lakes, usually within 100 miles (160 km) of the coast.

FEEDING: Harbor Seals feed primarily on fish, such as rockfish, cod, herring, flounder and salmon. To a lesser extent, they also feed on mollusks, such as clams, squid and octopus, and crustaceans, such as crabs, shrimp and crayfish. Newly weaned pups seem to

Northern Fur Seal

SIMILAR SPECIES: Northern Fur Seal (p. 112); Northern Sea-Lion (p. 114); Northern Elephant Seal (p. 126).

Northern Elephant Seal

Mirounga angustirostris

The aptly named Northern Elephant Seal is one of the largest seals of all—only its Southern Hemisphere counterpart, the Southern Elephant Seal (*Mirounga leonina*), is slightly larger.

The Northern Elephant Seal is an animal of superlatives, and it is also famous for its long migrations and incredible diving capabilities. The Northern Elephant Seal migrates twice a year, and some far-ranging males may cover 13,000 mi (21,000 km), which is even more than the renowned Gray Whale (p. 38), and spend more than 250 days at sea. When an elephant seal dives for food, it can remain submerged for 80 minutes and reach depths of up to 5000 ft (1500 m). Only the Sperm Whale (p. 106) and some of the beaked whales (pp. 94–101) can dive deeper or for longer.

Every year, sometime between December and March, adult Northern Elephant Seals arrive at sandy beaches in California or Mexico to give birth and mate. Northern Elephant Seals are very noisy on land: the

Male

Female

RANGE: These enormous seals are found from coastal Baja California to the Gulf of Alaska. They probably disperse a couple of hundred miles from the coast during the non-breeding season.

STATUS: Vulnerable but stable.

TOTAL LENGTH: male 12–16 ft (3.7–4.9 m); female 7–12 ft (2.1–3.7 m).

TOTAL WEIGHT: male up to 2½ tons (2300 kg); female 1 ton (910 kg).

SEALS & OTTERS

males produce a series of loud rattling snorts; the females make extremely inelegant sounds that resemble monstrous belches.

After pupping and mating, the adults and the young of the year depart for good feeding waters. Adult males and some juveniles may venture as far north as the Gulf of Alaska and the Aleutian Islands, where they feast on the abundant sea life. The females and most of the year's young do not travel quite as far: they prefer feeding in waters off Oregon and Northern California, between 40° N and 45° N.

Northern Elephant Seals feed in northern waters for two to five months before they return to the sandy shores of Mexico and California to molt sometime between April and August. When they molt, they shed their short, dense, yellowish-gray pelage along with large patches of old skin. During both the mating and molting seasons, elephant seals fast and lose up to 36 percent of their body weight. After the molting season, they once again venture out to food-rich waters to replenish their bodies before the mating season.

In the past, whalers frequently took high numbers of elephant seals in addition to their regular whale kills. This commercial harvest of elephant seals for oil reduced the worldwide population to between 100 and 1000 individuals, with some local populations completely extirpated. These seals are now fully protected under the Marine Mammal Protection Act, and their numbers have increased dramatically to a good population size. With increasing populations, more sightings off the Washington and Oregon coasts are being reported.

DESCRIPTION: Without a doubt, the sheer enormity of this creature gives away its identity. If you are in doubt, however, a closer look at its nose will be the confirmation: both sexes have a large nose that extends past the mouth, but adult males have a pendulous, inflatable, foot-long snout that resembles a trunk. This seal is mainly gray or light brown in color, with similarly colored sparse hair. Its hind flippers appear to be lobed on either side, and they have reduced claws. The tough skin of the male's neck and chest is covered with creases, scars and wrinkles, a feature absent in females. Pups are born black but molt to silver at one month.

cross over rocks to reach a sandy beach. This seal rarely hauls out during the feeding season; instead, it can rest at the surface of the water, and it can stay offshore for weeks at a time.

FEEDING: Elephant seals feed on a variety of sea creatures, including squid, octopus, small sharks, rays, pelagic red crabs and large fish. Adult males feed on larger prey than do the females and pups, and they typically migrate to more northern feeding grounds.

REPRODUCTION: The adults come ashore to give birth and mate sometime between December and March. These seals are polygamous, but not strongly territorial. Males arrive on shore first and battle fiercely for status in the social hierarchy. A high status means they can have a large harem. The females come ashore a couple of weeks after the males, and within a few days they may give birth to a pup conceived in the previous breeding season. The gestation period is 11 months. A female nurses her pup for no more than one month, during which time she fasts. Just a few days before her pup is to be weaned, she mates, and then, after she weans her pup, she leaves. Females are sexually mature at two to five years. Males typically cannot win a harem until they are 9 or 10 years old.

Northern Sea-Lion

HABITAT: The Northern Elephant Seal lives in the temperate waters of the Pacific Northwest. It migrates between its northern feeding waters and southern breeding and molting beaches twice a year. During its molting and breeding seasons, the Northern Elephant Seal hauls out onto sandy beaches. It does not haul out onto rocks, but it may

SIMILAR SPECIES:
Northern Sea-Lion (p. 114).

Sea Otter

Enhydra lutris

For many people, the playful and intelligent Sea Otter is among the most desired animals to see while visiting the Pacific Northwest. It has such a buoyant body and curious demeanor that watching it is not only comical but mesmerizing. When two Sea Otters are playing, they turn somersaults at the surface and wrestle together as if trying to dunk each other under. When they are resting, they lounge on their backs at the surface and rub their faces with curled-up paws, much like cats do when grooming. Sea Otters are even neighborly, and they regularly hobnob with sea-lions and seals.

The Sea Otter does not have a layer of insulating blubber like other marine mammals, and it relies on its high metabolism and thick coat to keep warm. Its full coat is both a blessing and a curse, however, because Sea Otters were hunted for their pelts almost to extinction. Remnant populations in remote parts of the Pacific Northwest became the stock for reintroduction programs that were necessary if the species was to survive. They now breed in pockets along the coast from California to Alaska and are slowly increasing their numbers, but they are still vulnerable. Sea Otters

RANGE: Sea Otters are found on the West Coast from southern California to the Aleutian Islands.

STATUS: Threatened (FWS) in some parts of its range; once critically endangered, but some populations have recovered.

TOTAL LENGTH: 30–60 in (76–152 cm).

TAIL LENGTH: 10–16 in (25–41 cm).

TOTAL WEIGHT: 50–100 lb (23–45 kg).

SEALS & OTTERS

can also be victims of oil spills, because the oil slicks their coat and destroys the insulating and water-proofing qualities of the fur. Otters caught in oil have extremely low chances of survival.

The Northern River Otter (p. 134) is the only animal you are likely to confuse with the Sea Otter, but the two are quite easy to tell apart—with the right information. Sea Otters do not venture more than 1 mi (1.6 km) out from shore, and they stay in water no more than 100 ft (30 m) deep. Typically, they stay close to rocky shores, anywhere kelp beds are abundant. They also prefer open coastlines, and are therefore rarely seen in the straits of northern Washington. Northern River Otters, on the other hand, are frequently seen in sheltered waters. Also, river otters are well-known for their travels, and an otter seen a few miles from shore, or that is swimming long distances from island to island, is most likely a Northern River Otter.

Anytime an otter is seen moving or eating on land, it is, again, a river otter. Sea Otters are very clumsy on land, and their locomotion is limited to an ungainly lope, an awkward walk or an even slower, body-dragging slide. Being so limited on land, the Sea Otter rarely comes out of the water, and only when a rough storm forces it out of its watery home.

DESCRIPTION: The stout-bodied Sea Otter has a short tail and a rounded head. Its slightly flattened tail is no more than one-third the length of its body. The fur may be a variety of colors, including light brown, reddish brown, yellowish gray or nearly black, and it is very thick, especially on the throat and chest. Folds of skin between the chest and each underarm form two pockets of skin. The head is often lighter than the body; in old males the head may be nearly white. The tiny ears may appear "pinched," but are otherwise inconspicuous. All four feet are webbed, and the hindlegs resemble flippers. Male Sea Otters are generally larger than females.

HABITAT: The Sea Otter lives almost its entire life at sea, only coming out onto rocks to rest during rough or stormy weather. It favors areas of kelp beds or reefs with nearby or underlying rocks. At night, or for daytime rest, a Sea Otter wraps itself in kelp at the surface. The kelp is attached under-

holds." To unload its pockets and eat, the otter rests on its back. It places the stone on its chest and uses it as an anvil on which to bash the shell of the urchin, shellfish or crustacean repeatedly until it breaks, exposing the flesh inside.

REPRODUCTION: Mating occurs in the water, usually in late summer. The female gives birth to one pup $6^{1}/_{2}$ to 9 months later. As in many weasels, delayed implantation of the embryo is probably involved in the long gestation period. On rare occasions, a female can have two pups. She gives birth in the water, and to nurse her young, she floats on her back and allows the pup to sit on her chest. The pup also plays and naps on its mother's chest. It is weaned when it is one year old, but it may stay with its mother for several more months, even if she gives birth again. If the mother senses danger, such as an approaching shark or Orca (p. 80), she will hold her pup under her forelegs and dive into a kelp bed until the danger passes.

water and prevents the otter from drifting while it sleeps. A Sea Otter is never more than 1 mi (1.6 km) from shore.

FEEDING: Sea Otters feed primarily on sea urchins, crustaceans, shellfish and fish. The otter dives underwater for up to five minutes and returns to the surface with its prey and a stone, using the pockets of skin that run from its chest to its underarms to carry its load. One otter was once seen unloading six urchins and three oysters from her "cargo

Northern River Otter

SIMILAR SPECIES:
Northern River Otter (p. 134).

Northern River Otter

Lontra canadensis

Many Northern River Otters live year-round on the coast, and enthusiastic wildlife watchers frequently mistake them for Sea Otters (p. 130). These two species have different appearances and preferred habitats, but they can be difficult to tell apart when they are seen in the water at a distance.

River otters can be active during day or night, but they tend to be more nocturnal where there is human activity. Their permanent dens are often in a bank, with both underwater and abovewater entrances.

DESCRIPTION: This large, weasel-like carnivore has a dark brown back that looks black when it is wet. It is paler below, and the throat is often silver gray. The head is broad and flattened, and it has small eyes, small ears and prominent, whitish whiskers. All four feet are webbed. The long tail is thick at the base and gradually tapers to the tip. Male river otters are larger than females.

HABITAT: River otters may visit coastal areas for brief periods, or they may live at the coast year-round. They sometimes roam

RANGE: The coastal range of the Northern River Otter extends from the Bering Strait to Northern California in the West, and from Labrador to Texas in the East.

STATUS: Threatened.

TOTAL LENGTH: 3½–4½ ft (1.1–1.4 m).

TAIL LENGTH: 12–20 in (30–51 cm).

TOTAL WEIGHT: 10–30 lb (4.5–14 kg).

far from water, especially young males establishing new territories. When roaming, a river otter rests under roots or overhangs, in hollow logs, in the abandoned burrows of other mammals or in ledges on rocky outcroppings.

FEEDING: On the coast, river otters feed primarily on crabs, although fish and shellfish are eaten when available. The coastal otters occasionally eat small terrestrial animals, such as mice, insects and earthworms.

REPRODUCTION: The female bears a litter of one to six blind, fully furred young in March or April. The young are 140 g (5 oz) at birth. They first leave the den at three to four months, and leave their parents at six to seven months. River otters become sexually mature at two years. The mother breeds again soon after her litter is born, but delayed implantation of the embryos puts off the birth until the following spring.

Sea Otter

SIMILAR SPECIES: Sea Otter (p. 130).

135

Glossary

AMPHIPODS: a group of shrimp-like creatures, including krill, that are the primary food for many whale species.

BALEEN: long, thin plates of keratinous material that hang from the upper jaw in a baleen whale's mouth and are used for filter-feeding.

BULL: an adult male cetacean or pinniped.

CALF: a baby cetacean.

CALLOSITY: an area of skin that is hardened by growths of lumpy, keratinous material.

CETACEAN: referring to the order of animals (Cetacea) that encompasses all whale, dolphin and porpoise species.

COPEPODS: a large group of marine and aquatic crustaceans, including amphipods, that are the primary food for many marine creatures.

COW: an adult female cetacean or pinniped.

ECHOLOCATION: the detection of an object by emitting sounds waves and interpreting the returning echoes, which are changed from bouncing off the object.

ENDANGERED: facing imminent extirpation or extinction.

EXTIRPATED: no longer existing locally, but found elsewhere in the world.

FLUKE: the horizontally flattened tail of a cetacean.

FUSIFORM: spindle-shaped; having an elongated body that tapers at both ends.

KERATINOUS: referring to the material that composes hair, wool and nails in many mammals.

KRILL: a general name to describe more than 80 species of small, shrimp-like organisms that are eaten by numerous marine creatures.

LARYNGEAL: referring to the larynx in the region of the throat, which can be made to vibrate to produce sound.

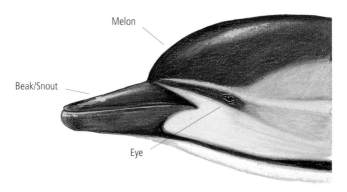

Melon

Beak/Snout

Eye

MIGRATION: the journey that an animal undergoes to get from one region to another, usually in response to seasonal and reproductive cycles.

MYSTICETES: all the cetaceans that have baleen instead of teeth.

NOMADIC: referring to creatures that move from region to region solely in response to food availability and that otherwise do not migrate.

ODONTOCETES: all the cetaceans that have teeth instead of baleen.

PELAGIC: living in the open sea far from land.

PINNIPEDIA: referring to the subgroup of carnivores (order Carnivora) that encompasses all seals, sea-lions and walruses.

PLANKTON: the tiny plants (phytoplankton) and animals (zooplankton) that drift in the water column and are the base of the food chain.

PUP: a baby pinniped.

PURSE-SEINE: a type of long net (often more than 1 mi [1.6 km] long) that is set around a large shoal of fish and drawn up from the bottom ropes to create a "purse" that traps the fish.

RORQUAL: strictly a whale in the genus *Balaenoptera*; most authorities also include the Humpback Whale.

ROSTRUM: the forward-projecting snout of a cetacean.

SONAR: the ability to detect or track objects underwater by monitoring their sound emissions or how sound bounces off them.

STRANDING: an event where a cetacean comes onto land or shallow water and becomes stuck; the reasons for such occurrences are unknown.

THREATENED: likely to become endangered if limiting factors are not reversed.

ULTRASOUND: ultrasonic sound waves that can penetrate surfaces to register subsurface details.

VESTIGIAL: a part or organ of a creature that has atrophied or is rendered functionless by the process of evolution.

VULNERABLE: of special concern because of characteristics that make it particularly sensitive to human activities or natural events.

Tail Stock   Keel   Dorsal Fin

Fluke

Eye

Belly

Rostrum

Flippers

Throat Pleats

Further Information

LOCAL RESEARCH AND CONSERVATION GROUPS

Oregon Coast Aquarium
2820 SE Ferry Slip Road
Newport, Oregon 97365
http://www.aquarium.org/

Point Defiance Zoo and Aquarium at Tacoma
5400 North Pearl Street
Tacoma, Washington 98407

The Whale Museum
62 First Street North
Friday Harbor, Washington 98250
http://www.whale-museum.org/

Mark O. Hatfield Marine Science Center
Oregon State University
2030 South Marine Science Drive
Newport, Oregon 97365

Center for Whale Research
1359 Smugglers Cove
Friday Harbor, Washington 98250

People for Puget Sound
1326 Fifth Avenue, Suite 450
Seattle, Washington 98101

Makah Cultural and Research Center
P.O. Box 160
Neah Bay, Washington 98357

EMERGENCY CONTACTS IN WASHINGTON AND OREGON

Washington sightings and strandings: (800) 562-8832

National Marine Fisheries Service, Washington
Harassment of Marine Mammals: (206) 3526-6133 or (360) 676-9268

Center for Whale Research, Washington
Harassment of Marine Mammals: (206) 378-5835

Whale Information, Oregon: (541) 563-2002

FURTHER READING

Boschung, H. T., Jr., J. D. Williams, D. W. Gotshall, D. K Caldwell and M. C. Caldwell. *National Audubon Society Field Guide to North American Fishes, Whales and Dolphins.* Alfred A. Knopf, New York.

Bulloch, D. K. 1993. *The Whaleswatcher's Handbook: A Guide to the Whales, Dolphins and Porpoises of North America.* Lyons and Burford, New York.

Byrd, E. 1995. *The Hello Dolphin Project.* World Dolphin Project. Dolphin Assisted Therapy 1995 Symposium, Cancun.

Carwardine, M. 1995. *Whales, Dolphins and Porpoises.* Stoddart Publishing, Toronto.

Carwardine, M., E. Hoyt, R. E. Fordyce and P. Gill. 1998. *Whales, Dolphins and Porpoises.* The Nature Company Guides, Time-Life Books, New York.

Clapham, P. 1997. *Whales.* Raincoast Books, Vancouver.

Conner, R. C., and D. M. Peterson. 1994. *The Lives of Whales and Dolphins.* Henry Holt and Company, New York.

Corrigan, P. 1991. *Where the Whales Are.* The Globe Pequot Press, Chester, Connecticut.

Darling, J. D., C. Nicklin, K. S. Norris, H. Whitehead and B. Würsig. 1995. *Whales, Dolphins and Porpoises.* National Geographic Society, Washington, D.C.

Flaherty, C. 1990. *Whales of the Northwest.* Cherry Lane Press, Seattle.

Gordon, D. G., and C. Flaherty. 1990. *Field Guide to the Orca.* Sasquatch Books, Seattle.

Kaiper, D., and N. Kaiper. 1978. *Tlingit: Their Art, Culture and Legends.* Hancock House Publishers, Saanichton, British Columbia.

Kaufman, G. D., and P. H. Forestell. 1986. *Hawaii's Humpback Whales.* Island Heritage Publishing, Hawaii.

Mason, A. 1999. *Whales, Dolphins and Porpoises.* Altitude Publishing, Canmore, Alberta.

Reader's Digest. 1997. *Reader's Digest Explores Whales, Dolphins and Porpoises.* The Reader's Digest Association, Pleasantville, New York.

Spalding, D. A. E. 1998. *Whales of the West Coast.* Harbour Publishing, Madeira Park, British Columbia.

Stewart, F., et al. *The Presence of Whales.* Whitecap Books, Vancouver/Toronto.

Stonehouse, B. 1998. *A Visual Introduction to Whales, Dolphins and Porpoises.* Checkmark Books, New York.

ONLINE INFORMATION

AMERICAN CETACEAN SOCIETY
http://www.acsonline.org/

CETACEA
http://www.cetacea.org/

COMMITTEE ON THE STATUS OF ENDANGERED WILDLIFE IN CANADA (COSEWIC)
http://www.cosewic.gc.ca/COSEWIC/

CONVENTION ON INTERNATIONAL TRADE OF ENDANGERED SPECIES OF WILD FLORA AND FAUNA (CITES)
http://www.wcmc.org.uk/CITES/eng/index.shtml

DOLPHIN RESEARCH CENTER
http://www.dolphins.org/

DOLPHIN INSTITUTE
http://www.dolphin-institute.com/

EARTHFILES
http://www.earthfiles.com/

INSTITUTE OF CETACEAN RESEARCH
http://www.whalesci.org/

Northern Fur Seal

INTERNATIONAL MARINE MAMMAL PROJECT
http://www.earthisland.org/immp/index.html

OCEAN LINK
http://www.oceanlink.island.net/olink.html

PROJECT AWARE
(Aquatic World Awareness, Responsibility and Education)
http://www.padi.com/

SEAL CONSERVATION SOCIETY
http://www.greenchannel.com/tec/species/

SHEDD AQUARIUM
http://www.sheddnet.org/

WHALE AND DOLPHIN CONSERVATION SOCIETY
http://www.wdcs.org/wdcs/index.htm

WHALENET
http://whale.wheelock.edu/

WHALES ON THE NET: LATEST NEWS
http://www.magna.com.au/NEWS/

Orca

Species Index

Page numbers in **boldface** type refer to the primary account for a species.